Wildness
Is All
Around Us

BY EUGENE KINKEAD

Spider, Egg and Microcosm
In Every War But One
A Concrete Look at Nature
Wildness Is All Around Us

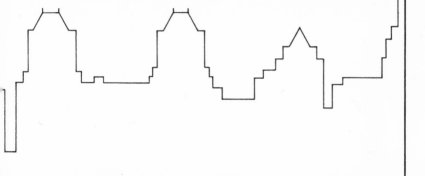

Wildness Is All Around Us

Notes of an Urban Naturalist

Eugene Kinkead, 1906

A Sunrise Book

E. P. DUTTON · NEW YORK

Grateful acknowledgment is given for permission to quote from "The Sparrow," William Carlos Williams, *Pictures from Brueghel and Other Poems.* Copyright 1955 by William Carlos Williams. Published by New Directions.

For information contact: E. P. Dutton, 2 Park Avenue,
New York, N.Y. 10016
Portions of this book previously appeared in The New Yorker *in slightly different form.*

Library of Congress Cataloging in Publication Data
[Library of Congress Catalog Number]

Kinkead, Eugene, 1906-
Wildness is all around us.

"A Sunrise book."
1. Urban ecology (Biology)—United States. I. Title.
QH541.5.C6K56   500.9'173'2   78-1406

ISBN: 0-87690-277-8

Published simultaneously in Canada by Clarke, Irwin & Company Limited,
Toronto and Vancouver

Production by Stuart Horowitz

Designed by The Etheredges

10   9   8   7   6   5   4   3   2   1

First Edition

Contents

Foreword

The urbanized portions of our land hold the majority of our people. Nearly 170 million of our 225 million population live in our central cities, on their fringes, or in the wider districts beyond, those compact plats of suburbia that form the outer marches of our metropolitan areas. In our rural neighborhoods, where nature walks hand in hand with daily life, only a relatively minor fraction of our citizens, some 55 million, call these places home.

In the urban sections, nature tends to be forgotten. Along many blocks, for instance, deep within our central cities' slough, the moon is almost never seen. Residents there, when dark falls, rarely look aloft. Man-erected walls allow them a view of only narrow strips of sky. Besides, many feel too much is going on at night to bother an intentional glance upward. Neon signs glow. Pavements resound with footsteps. Electronic media crackle. Man, active in his tiny concerns, is everywhere. So the pale and lovely light of the moon silvers empty rooftops.

Yet despite such inattention by our city dwellers, nature irresistibly rules them. It provides the air they breathe (and their bodily reaction to its pollution) . . . the rain that wets them . . . the sun that makes the daylight come. Far more obdurate and persistent than anything that man can devise, it encompasses them all. And it is very strong. Witness some of its more violent expressions—a volcanic eruption submerging a town, a vast tidal wave sloshing across hundreds of miles of open ocean toward defenseless isles, or the terrifying impact, stronger than either of these, of a stone-and-iron meteorite striking the earth, such as the one that earlier in this century buried itself in a Siberian forest with a tremor felt as far away as London. Had it fallen on Manhattan, Manhattan Island would have disappeared.

Nature's handiwork, fearsome or beguiling, is always artless. Man's is just the opposite. The objects he makes, the trappings of his civilization, are fabricated from materials brought under his control, things he has tamed. Nature's doings, by contrast, are never so.

Many of its minor displays are understandably overlooked. Nevertheless, these aspects of nature's ceaseless drama are often fascinating. City dwellers in particular, who live where nature frequently marches veiled, reading what follows will, like me, I hope, find some charm in these accounts of an Arctic bird's mistake; the rediscovery of a long-lost tree; a rock record of ages past, framed in a metropolitan setting; wildflowers abloom amid traffic fumes; the coyote's continental spread; and the worldwide saga of the house sparrow.

Colebrook, Connecticut
September 1977

Wildness
Is All
Around Us

Steller's Eider

From a stark region north of the Arctic Circle, a breath of wildness touched down last spring within our country's temperate borders. An exotic avian waif, unexpected and uninvited, it was sighted off the coast of the sovereign state of Massachusetts, a commonwealth that over the years has had, perhaps, more than its share of odd birds, human as well as avian. Prominent among the latter, all notably displaced members of the biological class Aves, have been, in chronological order of their appearance over the last century, the Eurasian kestrel, the white-tailed eagle, the black-tailed godwit, and, several years ago, the Eurasian curlew. None of these has been reported from anywhere else on the North American continent.

The odd bird immediately under consideration arrived last year shortly after the advent of calendar spring and settled snugly into the Atlantic Ocean off the shore of Scituate, a suburban community some fifteen miles southeast of Boston. It was a Steller's eider, a sea duck commonest along the northern coast of Siberia, where most of the world's estimated 400,000 Steller's eiders are to be found. A few range as far west as western Europe, where they are partial to the picturesque fjords of Norway. In the United States they are normally present—and in rather sparse numbers only—along the Arctic Ocean and Bering Sea shorelines of Alaska, where they breed, and off the Alaska Peninsula and Aleutian Islands, where they winter.

The newcomer was discovered at 10:30 A.M. on Tuesday, March 29, last year, by Robert Vernon, of Westwood, a Boston suburb to the west of Scituate, and his son, James, who had arrived that morning from his home in Connecticut for a familial visit. The two Vernons are both ardent birders, which is the customary name for the growing group in this country of those who make a hobby of observing birds. The two decided, simply out of the usual ornithological curiosity, to sally forth that morning by automobile and see what species they might turn up along the Boston South Shore. When they spotted the eider off Scituate, they were astounded, but they were also ecstatic. From the data in their bird guides, they were sure they had a Steller's. Although they continued to bird in the area, they drove along with, at the same time, an eye to finding a roadside pay telephone. When they did, at about noon, they immediately put in a call about their find to Richard Forster, the head of the natural history section at the Massachusetts Audubon Society's headquarters in Lincoln, a community to the west of Boston. Forster, elated but necessarily professionally cautious, was first of all anxious to confirm the news. He accordingly reached a long-experienced birder, Wayne Peterson, a biology teacher in a junior high school in the Boston suburb of Hanover, and asked him to go down to the shore and check things out. By five that afternoon, Forster received word from Peterson that there was, indeed, a Steller's eider, a male, floating in the waters off Scituate.

The bird is only the second of its kind to show up off the

eastern coast of the United States and the only one to remain alive very long. The first, also a male, was spied in the township of Scarborough in southern Maine in 1926, in company with several old squaws, another variety of sea duck. It was collected (euphemism for shot) for identification purposes. A third record of this eider off the eastern coast is now considered erroneous. In January some ten years ago a hunter in Maryland gunned down three fowl out of a flock of eight. One bore a band that, when computerized, seemingly belonged to a Steller's eider on which it had been placed five years before at Izenbek Bay, Alaska. It is now believed that, by mistake, some of the digits of the band's number were transposed when put into the computer and that all the hunter's quarry were canvasback ducks, a species that regularly winters in the Chesapeake Bay area.

With positive identification of the vagrant having been established, the society's next move was to alert the community of birders, both near and far. This spirit of mutual assistance traditionally animates that close-knit company and is known as the birders' grapevine. The network that, with blinding speed, flashes political rumors through our nation's capital rivals, but does not surpass, in pace that which is operated by the birders. Officials at the society at once called friends whom they knew had birder friends. But this was merely the beginning. Mainly the dissemination of the news came through broadcasting. Word of the eider was put on the "Voice of Audubon," a taped message that can be heard by calling a Boston telephone number; it provides data on what rare or interesting birds are then to be found in or around the city. The Boston tape is merely one of eighteen such recordings presenting similar ornithological information that can be heard in communities across the country. One of these, the New York City "Rare Bird Alert," promptly incorporated tidings of the eider, and it is believed that several of the others did so as well. Being on the telephone, the messages are available twenty-four hours a day.

The next morning the society undertook another precautionary move. It wanted to assure itself that the bird was wild. Exotic birds have been known to appear in nature following escapes from zoos or from the aviaries of dealers and private hobbyists. Accordingly, Forster got in touch with Dick Ryan, the director of the Turtle Back Zoo in West Orange, New Jersey. Ryan is probably the nation's authority on exotic escaped birds. Forster asked him about the likelihood of the Steller's eider's being an escapee. Ryan was sure it was not. He said there was no record that the species had ever passed through the Department of Agriculture's bird quarantine station maintained near him at Clifton, New Jersey. This is where foreign birds brought in for dealers and hobbyists must spend a month to be sure they are free of disease. No Steller's eider had been recorded as in confinement in the country. The reason, Ryan went on, was simple. In his opinion, the Steller's eider would be impossible to keep alive in a cage. Therefore, the Scituate bird, he stated, must be wild.

Reaction to the news of the eider was swift. The day after its discovery birders by the dozen were already at the Scituate shore. During the period of its stay, the number mounted into the high hundreds. Telephone calls came in to the society and to local birders from as far away as Wisconsin and Arizona. Enthusiasts converged from every state in New England and from New York, New Jersey, Pennsylvania, Maryland, the District of Columbia, Virginia, and Ohio, not to mention the Canadian province of Ontario. Those coming from a distance, feeling that time was of the essence in such a situation, usually flew in and, after hiring cars in Boston to get to Scituate, strode along the shore, peering contentedly at the eider through an array of expensive field glasses and telescopes. The National Audubon Society, whose headquarters are in New York City, estimates the country has 200,000 to 300,000 dedicated birders, generally people of more than adequate means, who spend half a billion dollars a year on such appurtenances of their pastime as costly cameras, optical goods, and profusely illustrated volumes. That many of them traveled by airplane to see a rare duck should come as no surprise.

Among those who arrived on the beach at Scituate were a New Haven, Connecticut, housewife; a male employee of the New York State Department of Transportation, based in Albany; and a Philadelphia lawyer, accompanied by three officials of the Academy of Natural Sciences, a research organization in that city, who could be expected to note appreciatively a relatively uncommon member of the biological branch of the natural sciences. Mr. and Mrs. Robert Shaper, of Cleveland, also saw the bird. They were in Boston at the time and had, as birders customarily do, called the "Voice of Audubon." Hearing of the duck's presence, they hurriedly hired a car and drove to Scituate. The interest also penetrated to the upper echelons of our government. The office of the nation's energy czar, Dr. James Schlesinger, a veteran bird-watcher, called the Massachusetts Audubon Society's headquarters to check if the Steller's eider was actually present. Apparently, however, Dr. Schlesinger became too involved in Washington to make the jaunt northward and add the bird to his life list.

The life list is a record of the different species a birder has seen during the course of his hobby. The usual reason a birder goes out of his way to see a rare bird is to add it to his life list. Consequently, listing has become the great beating heart of birding, holding many of its practitioners in the grip of a passion that in some cases approaches frenzy. It is, at its height, an urge as strong as, although considerably less debilitating than, alcohol addiction or compulsive gambling.

For most birders in this country the important section of the life list is that for North American birds. The present, and greatly envied, holder of the record for this category is Joseph W. Taylor, of Honeoye Falls, New York. His North American list consists of 721 species of birds that have been accorded full species rank by the American Ornithologists' Union. This scholarly body gives as 685 in number the species that are known to reside in, or regularly visit, North America. Taylor has seen all of these. The rest on his list are accidentals, alien birds that have arrived in North America by chance. Taylor saw his first Steller's eider ten years ago in Hooper Bay north of the delta of the Yukon River in Alaska. Therefore, he did not zip over to Scituate last year. However, he can be quickly mobile when necessary, as was the case, for example, five years ago when he flew 2,000 miles from Phoenix, Arizona, to the Florida Keys to bag a pair of male accidentals— the loggerhead kingbird and the stripe-headed tanager. Both live in the Caribbean and the Greater Antilles area. The former, wearing a dingy gray or brown coat with yellow crown patch, is about the size of a robin. The latter, the size of a large sparrow, has a white-striped black head, black-and-white wings, and a yellow breast.

Myron Litchfield, of Norwell, a town only several miles from Scituate, accepted the request of the Massachusetts Audubon Society to monitor the continued presence of the eider. This was to keep information current on the "Voice of Audubon" tape. Its content is revised each Monday, Wednesday, and Friday. Litchfield, an experienced birder, checked the duck at least morning and evening every weekday and oftener on the weekend. A few years ago in the same area, he took a photograph of a Mississippi kite, the first positive record of this bird for the East Coast. The photograph was so clear that collection of the bird was not necessary. During Litchfield's trips to the shore, he noted that the eider, which stayed along a five-mile stretch of the coast, was very cooperative. It swam in the water from 200 feet to half a mile out, rather close for a marine species, keeping company with a flock of common goldeneyes, another sort of sea duck. This was the case despite the fact that there were plenty of common eiders nearby. Therefore, on the basis of the actions of Steller's eider here and at Scarborough, Maine, where the bird also appeared to prefer the companionship of noneiders to that of the many common eiders about, it would appear that the species avoids other eiders, opting instead, at least on visits to our East Coast, to associate with sea ducks not eiders.

Steller's eider is the trimmest, the fastest flying, and the smallest of the four eiders to be found in North America. But it is not a really small bird. It is diminutive only in comparison with the other heavier, more clumsily built eiders. It is about the size of, but somewhat heavier than, a wood duck, being a foot and a half long, weighing two pounds, and having a wing spread of thirty inches. In flight, the wings whistle.

The male is a striking-looking bird, almost impossible to confuse with any other. A black patch, which surrounds a yellowish green or light olive eye, lies in the center of a shiny white head. A black collar low on the neck continues down the back as a black line. The chest and sides are cinnamon buff, deepening to orange on the breast with the center of the breast sepia. The female, a shade smaller than the male, is far less colorful. She is clad merely in tones of variegated brown with small blue oblongs on the wing, like a mallard. Both sexes have a slight crest at the back of the head.

Litchfield reported that the eider was an avid feeder. Frequently it tipped up in the water in the characteristic foraging posture of ducks. Sometimes, for appreciable periods, it dived below the surface. Mollusks, crustaceans, and small fishes are its main food. The bill is strong enough to crush the thin shells of razor clams and mussels, which are items in its diet. It pursues and captures small fishes by swimming underwater, using both its webbed feet and wings in the chase.

Steller's eider is named for Georg Wilhelm Steller (originally Stöhler), who was born in Germany in 1709, the son of an organist. Thirty-seven years later, he died in Siberia following a thirteen-year period of employment for the rulers of Russia, first the Empress Anna and then her successor the Empress Elizabeth, in the beginning as an army physician and then as explorer-scientist. This was at a time when the original thirteen colonies that were to begin our nation were still closely attached to Great Britain. Steller was an irascible person, but an energetic and indomitable field worker. Called the pioneer of Alaskan natural history, he was the first white man to step ashore there. That was in 1741. Vitus Bering, for whom the Bering Sea is named, was in command of the Russian ship *Saint Peter,* to which Steller was attached as naturalist. After a long and wandering journey over the fog-laden waters of the North Pacific, Bering at last discovered the western coast of North America, for which he had been searching, making a landfall on that part of it which was later to be incorporated into our forty-ninth state. Steller was in the initial rowboat sent ashore to the new land by the *Saint Peter.* When it beached on Kayak Island in the panhandle of Alaska, Steller was the first to leap out, completely obsessed by his desire to begin observing and collecting.

While there, he noted a sizable blue jay, larger than our eastern species, with a purplish crest and mantle. This is now known as Steller's jay. It is an inhabitant of the Rockies and, westward, of coniferous forests. At least four other animals, three of them still in existence, are named for Steller. Those yet alive are Steller's sea eagle, a large fish-eating bird with white shoulders, rump, and tail that dwells on the western shore of the North Pacific, Steller's sea lion, the largest of the five species of sea lions, whose males reach a length of eleven feet and weigh a ton, and Steller's albatross, sometimes called the short-tailed albatross, a great, largely white seabird of the North Pacific. The extinct creature is Steller's sea cow, an enormous beast twenty-five feet long, with small head, no teeth, and a tail with horizontal flukes. It vanished toward the end of the eighteenth century from its range in the North Pacific.

Besides being an avid feeder, the eider, Litchfield noticed, was also an avid Lothario. Throughout the period of its stay, it assiduously courted a female goldeneye. Normally, different species of animals are reproductively isolated. Under ordinary circumstances, therefore, they do not hybridize. However, exceptions do occur. These are fairly common among waterfowl. For example, the mallard mates with both the black and pintail duck, and the offspring are fertile. Male ducks, the theory is, often cannot recognize the drab females of their own species. Thus they go into their wooing routine on a chance basis, adopting the theory, apparently, that naught can be lost and perhaps something gained. Female ducks, however, are programmed to recognize the courtship ritual of their species' males. As a consequence, the Steller's eider throughout the duration of its suit received only cool glances from the object of its affection. Nevertheless, it persisted gallantly through the evening of April 8, Litchfield reported. On the morning of April 9, Litchfield found that the Steller's eider, after a sojourn of eleven days, had departed. Even an amorous visitor from Siberia presumably can, in time, take a hint.

Not Extinct, After All

Sometimes the wild takes back its own—sometimes forever, sometimes only for a spell. This is the tale of a rare wildling. It was discovered, then lost. For many years it was actually believed to be extinct, gone forever into that void, the realm of died-out biota, which has swallowed up so many other forms of life. But, in the end, this proved to be untrue.

Let us start at the beginning.

Public Law 93-205, which is better known as the Endangered Species Act of 1973 and was passed by Congress on December 28 of that year, directed the secretary of the Smithsonian Institution of Washington, D.C., to prepare, by the end of 1974, a report on

9

United States plants that had recently become extinct or were deemed to be in danger of becoming so before long. The report, a monumental job of research, surveying the status of some 20,000 plants in the forty-nine continental states (Hawaii was dealt with separately) and making recommendations for safeguarding those in jeopardy, was successfully turned out, in the designated but brief time, under the supervision of Dr. Edward S. Ayensu, the chairman of the Smithsonian's botany department. Of the flora listed, some 10 percent, or 2,099 species, was found either to be in real danger or to have lately departed. In all, 761 plants were designated as "endangered," meaning their survival was in serious doubt; 1,238 were listed as "threatened"; and an even 100 were declared extinct—at least in the wild.

Of those plants labeled extinct, only two were among the largest—the trees. One of these, the "lost" *Franklinia* (*Franklinia alatamaha*), is a rather famous species in the world of botany. It was discovered during Colonial days: John Bartram, King's Botanist, and his son, Wiilliam, found it in the year 1765 growing beside the Altamaha River, on the low coastal plain of southeast Georgia, in what is now McIntosh County, about thirty miles from the sea. Its finders described it as a shrub or small tree reaching a maximum height of thirty-odd feet, and they correctly placed it in the tea family. It had glossy green leaves somewhat resembling those of the magnolia. The large creamy white flowers, renewing themselves in warm weather for weeks and even months, had the fragrance of orange blossoms. The original population is believed to have occupied a locale no larger at best than five acres, a tract of acid land composed of sandhill bog. The tree, the only species in its genus, was named in honor of Benjamin Franklin, in 1785, five years before he died. In 1803, a botanist reported only six or eight mature examples of *Franklinia* left at the original site, though many cultivated examples were by then flourishing elsewhere. By 1806, no more were to be seen in the wild. Why the species vanished from its native habitat is uncertain. One theory is that the alkaline Altamaha River flooded the area, doing the plant in. A more likely cause, however, botanists think, is overcollecting. Soon after the discovery of *Franklinia*, the Bartrams, recognizing the tree's decorative qualities, began digging up specimens and dispatching them to Philadelphia and elsewhere. This practice was continued for decades by others. It produced at least one benefit. Now the tree, although it is gone from nature, exists quite widely in arboretums, public grounds, and gardens in both the Old World and the New. In fact, three rather scraggly examples stand before the National Museum of Natural History in Washington—the Smithsonian building where the report on endangered flora was put together. A much more impressive representative, about twenty-five feet high, rises on the Senate side of the Capitol grounds.

The other tree on the extinct list was not a famous one. Nor did it have the early good fortune to be preserved by being planted in gardens. Indeed, in recent years botanists had begun to question seriously whether such a tree had ever existed. It was a birch, sometimes known as Ashe's birch. It was discovered in 1914 by William Willard Ashe, an experienced forester employed by the United States Forest Service, on the banks of a modest stream draining a part of Smyth County, in the rural, mountainous region of southwest Virginia—a section of the Appalachians that Ashe knew well. Some time later, Ashe, following scientific custom, sent materials from the tree—twigs, leaves, and female catkins (which bear the seeds)—to the United States National Herbarium, at the Smithsonian; to the New York Botanical Garden; and to two botanical adjuncts of Harvard University—the Arnold Arboretum, in Jamaica Plain, Massachusetts, and the Gray Herbarium, in Cambridge. Accompanying the specimens were labels in Ashe's handwriting stating that the tree, from twenty to twenty-five feet high, was found in the month of June 1914, on the banks of Dickey Creek, in Smyth County, at an altitude of 2,800 feet, south of the Sugar Grove Station. This building, now vanished, was a depot of the Marion and Rye Valley Railroad, erected at a time when rail lines penetrated even to sections that were very sparsely populated, as Dickey Creek then was and still is. The tree, Ashe thought, resembled the black, or sweet, birch, also found in the area, both having a black, aromatic bark with a wintergreen fragrance and flavor. The leaves of the two trees, however, were different. Black birch leaves are pointed, like an arrowhead; those of Ashe's birch were rounded at the tip. In a paper published four years after his find—in the April 1918 issue of *Rhodora,* the journal of the New England Botanical Club—Ashe formally named the tree *Betula lenta uber* n. var. (meaning "new variety," thus indicating that he believed it to be a new variety of the very common black birch). *Betula lenta* is the name of the black birch, and *uber* is the Latin word for "fruitful" (rather a strange epithet, as it later turned out, to tie to this tree); a variety is a biological form whose differences within the species are too slight to entitle it to true specific rank. Among the facts about the tree in the *Rhodora* article were the length and breadth of the leaf, the number of primary veins, and other leaf characteristics; the length of the leaf stalk; and peculiarities of the female catkins, fruit scales, and seeds. The tree was one of more than 100 new species and varieties that Ashe botanically described and named in some forty years as a state and federal forester—a career that started in 1893 in North Carolina, where he was born. He placed the birch in a group (series Costate) that includes the black birch and the yellow birch (*Betula alleghaniensis*), both widely found in the Dickey Creek area.

The tree stayed in that niche for less than thirty years. In 1945, Dr. Merritt Lyndon Fernald, Fisher Professor of Natural History at Harvard, director of its Gray Herbarium, and one of the most eminent American botanists of this century, took a new look at the birches of eastern North America, and in the process his eye fell on *Betula lenta uber.* After seeing Ashe's specimens from both Harvard sources, Fernald, writing in the October 1945 issue of *Rhodora,* raised the tree to full specific rank, calling it simply *Betula uber.* In his opinion, the plant, except for its aromatic bark, had little in common with the black birch. Because of the structure of its leaves and female catkins, it more nearly resembled, he thought, the birches in series Humiles—a group that includes the low, or swamp, birch (*Betula pumila*), a plant of the northeastern United States and Canada, which, in its more northerly habitat, is sometimes a dwarf only a foot or two high. Since Fernald's pronouncement, Ashe's birch has remained a full species in series Humiles, although it appears to be widely separated in structure and habitat from the other members of the series and is the only one not found readily in nature.

Within a few years, a research fellow at Harvard decided to investigate this scarcity; Albert G. Johnson, a horticulturist, until recently with the University of Minnesota, was one of a number of botanists to search, over the years, for a specimen of Ashe's birch. In the winter of 1953, Johnson, supported by funds from the Maria Moors Cabot Foundation for Botanical Research at Harvard University, traveled to Dickey Creek—a watercourse that flows north through the little community of Sugar Grove into the South Fork of the Holston River, which, as a tributary of the Tennessee River, is part of the Mississippi River drainage system. Although the leaves were off the trees at the time of Johnson's visit, he wrote, in the June 1954 issue of *Rhodora,* that he felt he would have had no difficulty recognizing *Betula uber* if it had been present in any quantity in the area. Johnson walked south from Sugar Grove along the banks of the creek. Near town, he reported, these banks were mainly clear but occasionally bore an irregular fringe of shrubs and some trees. He pursued his search over a stretch of four miles, going well into the hilly region of the 617,533-acre Jefferson National Forest, through which the southern portion of Dickey Creek runs. He mounted considerably higher than the 2,800 feet at which Ashe said he had found the tree. But Johnson saw only black and yellow birches—the common ones thereabouts. Nor could the district ranger in the national forest, whom Johnson had queried and who had looked for the tree himself, give Johnson any leads.

Accordingly, in the last paragraph of his article Johnson wrote that the birch "probably no longer exists as an individual and very likely never did so in the form of a population. Ashe's birch has probably died or been destroyed in the process of urbanization of the community in which he found it forty years ago. It is probable that this birch variety was founded solely on an aberrant individual and certainly does not appear to deserve further consideration as a species." End of article. By that time, many botanists were of the opinion that, for some unaccountable reason, the tree might have been a freak.

Here the matter rested, in limbo, until the beginning of this decade. In the early 1960s, Peter Mazzeo, a research assistant at the United States National Arboretum, a unit of the Department of Agriculture, who was working on a proposed flora of Virginia, came upon the written spoor of *Betula uber* and found himself fascinated by reports of the discovery and subsequent apparent evaporation into thin air of Ashe's birch. In 1970, he decided to examine all the material from the tree that he could get his hands on and to study everything available on it in print. Besides the material Ashe had sent to the four herbaria, four other sets of botanical specimens had turned up in Ashe's effects following his death in 1932. These went to his alma mater, the University of North Carolina, which is presumed to have sent one to the Carnegie Museum of Natural History, in Pittsburgh and one to the herbarium at the National Arboretum.

Altogether, Mazzeo was able to look at seven of Ashe's specimens—the four from the institutions that had received them after Ashe's death, plus three of the original four sent out by Ashe in 1914. The latter were those at the Gray Herbarium, the Arnold Arboretum, and the New York Botanical Garden. The material sent to the Smithsonian had been lost, and lost rather early. In a letter written in 1922, Ashe complained he had been unable to find the material he had shipped to the institution. The specimen sent there was designated the primary type (or holotype, meaning the single specimen designated by an author as the type of a species at the time of establishing the group) for *Betula uber*. Thus when Fernald wrote his paper, he had to base his observations on a duplicate (or isotype), selecting the one at the Gray Herbarium, which Mazzeo has since designated as the replacement for the lost holotype.

During his research, however, Mazzeo was able to find an eighth set of specimens, which had gone all but unnoticed for years. Searching the files of the Arnold Arboretum herbarium, he found a set of material on Ashe's birch with a label, in handwriting different from Ashe's, that said the specimen had been collected by H. B. Ayres on Cressy Creek. This stream is not far to the east of Dickey Creek and, like it, feeds into the South Fork of the Holston River. Also on the label were the words *"Betula uber"* in Fernald's unmistakable script. According to Fernald's custom, his notation was undated. The assumption is that before writing his paper he had requested all birch materials from the

Arnold to be sent to him at Gray, had seen the Ayres specimen, had annotated the label, and had forgotten about it by the time he wrote his paper.

Ayres, an older man than Ashe by sixteen years, was a forester usually employed by private industry. He worked largely for railroads, appraising the timber on their lands; that is, he was what was known in the trade as a "timber cruiser." He was also an occasional collaborator of Ashe's. Among their joint works was a 1905 report for the United States Geological Survey entitled *The Southern Appalachian Forests*. In it they evaluated the timber possibilities of the Dickey and Cressy creek districts, among other areas. The report made no reference to *Betula uber*.

In 1973, in an article dealing with the dozen-odd species of the birch family present in Virginia, Mazzeo made brief mention of the mysteries of *Betula uber*. He mentioned the name Cressy Creek in print for the first time, albeit almost peripherally (and the paper misspelled it "Creesy"). The item was published in a quarterly called *Jeffersonia: A Newsletter of Virginia Botany*. A year and a half later, in the September 1974 number of the botanical quarterly *Castanea*, edited at the University of West Virginia, Mazzeo devoted an entire paper, with photographic illustrations of *Betula uber* material, to what he had been able to learn in his several years' study of the birch. The paper noted that, after sixty years and many searches, no trace of living specimens of this shadowy plant had been found.

Mazzeo himself, meanwhile, tried to rectify this lack. He had made a special trip to the region solely to search for Ashe's birch. This turned out to be just another unsuccessful effort. But in February 1975 the *Christian Science Monitor* carried a feature on Mazzeo's search for Ashe's birch, which I happened to see. As a result, I telephoned Mazzeo and said that if he planned another hunt I would like to go along. In my layman's ignorance, I said that if the tree had been found once, I thought it certainly could be found again. Mazzeo said that, as a matter of fact, he was planning another trip in the fall and would be glad to have me accompany him.

In the meantime, a reading of Mazzeo's 1973 paper had interested a Virginia native named Douglas Ogle, then twenty-six years old. He was a biology instructor at Virginia Highlands Community College, in nearby Abingdon, and was also in the Ph.D. program in botany at Virginia Polytechnic Institute and State University, in Blacksburg. When Mazzeo's piece on the birch came out in *Castanea,* Ogle decided to map out a careful campaign of search for the tree and to follow it in his 1975 summer vacation. His plan was a sensible one. Both Ashe and Ayres had reported their finds along the two creeks. Ogle decided that the tree, as a biological entity, might be restricted to such locales. Therefore, he thought there were a couple of likely ways in which the birch could have been discovered. Since there were only two access routes to the area, it could have been by someone walking along the railroad tracks, whose right-of-way cut back and forth across the streams, or by someone moving along the local wagon roads, now also out of use in most cases, in the areas adjacent to the creeks.

On August 22, 1975, Ogle found, growing among ordinary black birches along the west bank of Cressy Creek, on the property of Garland Ross, a retired schoolteacher and part-time farmer, a number of birches with odd-looking leaves. With Ross's permission, he collected some leafy twigs from the unusual plants. That same day, Ogle took his materials to the herbarium at Virginia Polytechnic Institute, where Leonard Uttal, the herbarium's assistant curator, studied the find using Fernald's 1945 article and Mazzeo's article, with its photographs, detailed descriptions, and measurements. On August 28, Uttal got Mazzeo on the telephone in Washington. "I think *Betula uber* has been found," Uttal said.

Plans were immediately begun for an expedition to determine whether this was so and also to seek other specimens—some of them, preferably, small enough to use for nursery purposes. Mazzeo notified his superior, Dr. F. G. Meyer, supervisory research botanist at the National Arboretum, who, not surprisingly, wanted to come along. I was alerted and happily agreed to appear. So, with the same result, were Ogle and Dr. W. H. Wagner, Jr., who became the group leader by virtue of his early interest in the plant and his professional eminence. He was then chairman of the Department of Botany of the University of Michigan, at Ann Arbor, and then and now a professor in its School of Natural

Resources (of which the forestry division is a part), a well-known specialist in the field of ferns, and a highly respected general botanist. For some months previously, he had been talking with Mazzeo about going with him in a search for *Betula uber*. The trip was set for mid-September.

On the appointed day, our contingent gathered, late in the afternoon, at the airport at Roanoke, Virginia. Wagner proved to be an acute, animated scholar in his middle fifties, with an easy social manner; Meyer, tall and spare, is about the same age; and Mazzeo, bearded and soft-spoken, is in his thirties. These last two had motored down that day from Washington in a panel van bearing the logo of the Department of Agriculture. In the back of the van were various pieces of equipment, such as plant presses with felt blotters; newsprint, in which to press the specimens; cardboard ventilators, to hold them; and a pruner about twenty feet long, for reaching remote twigs on a tree. Because only federal employees are allowed to ride in a government vehicle, I rented a car at the airport, and Wagner and I followed the others, in their van, over a stretch of about 100 miles to Marion, which is the seat of Smyth County. (The town is named after the Revolutionary general Francis Marion, known as the Swamp Fox.) There we were to spend the next couple of nights in a motel. Ogle was to meet us the following day.

At dinner that evening, to my considerable surprise, Wagner gave what was almost a lecture downgrading the chances of our project. He argued—quite convincingly, it seemed to me—that the tree we were about to see might well not be what we thought it was. Playing the part of devil's advocate, he brought up numerous reasons to suppose that it was a botanical aberration, not worthy of species rank—if, indeed, it was Ashe's birch at all. Perhaps, however, his stand was to have been expected. At the University of Michigan, I had learned, the botanists and the foresters had long questioned the existence of *Betula uber*. For one thing, in the summer of 1952 Walter F. Kleinschmidt, of the University of Michigan's Botanical Gardens, had carefully searched the area in Smyth County where Ashe had reported his birch and had been unable to find any trace of it. At the end of Wagner's talk, the two other botanists disagreed with his objections. "We think the tree is as advertised," Mazzeo said. "I predict that tomorrow four new pairs of eyes will see *Betula uber*."

One thing the three botanists agreed upon completely was that if the object of our trip were generally known other botanists by the dozen would be camping around us in no time. As a matter of fact, our party, to my surprise, was substantially increased next morning. Following an early breakfast, we left the motel in the two cars under an iron-gray sky a little before eight for a rendezvous with Ogle at a point about halfway along the road that runs between Marion and Sugar Grove, a community in the hill country, about a dozen miles to the southeast of the county seat. At the appointed place, we met Ogle, a tall, heavyset, quiet man, who was alone in his car. Almost immediately, another automobile, with Leonard Uttal and Dr. Duncan Porter, a systemic botanist at Virginia Polytechnic Institute, joined us; then came a third car, carrying two members of the biology department of Virginia Highlands Community College, where Ogle taught. A few minutes later, our caravan of five vehicles, led by Ogle, set off for the site on Cressy Creek where he had found the birch.

Along the way, it started to rain a little. Tropical storm Eloise at the time was bringing inclement weather and, indeed, floods to much of the East. After a drive of about ten minutes, we stopped south of Sugar Grove and parked along the shoulder of a blacktop road. The road ran along Cressy Creek, which bore on each bank a thin fringe of trees. As I glanced around me, I could see that we were at the bottom of a deep, overgrown valley. Empty, tree-covered hills rose on either side of us. The farmhouse of Garland Ross lay ahead to our right; that of Ray Haulsee, behind to our left; both farms were adjacent to the boundaries of the Jefferson National Forest. The sounds of pigs and chickens and, from time to time, the lowing of cows could be heard. The rain, borne on flurries of wind, was heavier now.

The nine of us left our cars and, with Ogle in the lead, made our way through the roadside screen of trees to Cressy Creek. "Most of what we're looking for is on the other side," Ogle said. The stream was about fifteen feet wide and nine to twelve inches deep, and was strewn with rocks. We crossed by wading or leaping cautiously from rock to rock. When all of us had reached the west bank and were among the trees, Ogle suggested we look up. "Can you see leaves that are dissimilar to those of the black birch?" he asked. The leaves of the black birch were numerous all around us, but when I looked up, it was hard, with the rain pelting into my face, to see anything. Then Wagner, standing beside a nearby tree, cried elatedly, "Yes, yes, I see what you mean. The rounded leaf! The rounded leaf!" And, following his gaze, I saw what he saw—leaves formed like old-fashioned palm-leaf fans ranged in serried ranks above his head. That was the shape of the leaf that had been depicted in Mazzeo's article. After more than sixty years of botanical mystery, of doubts, of denials and fears of extinction, the living flora grew at mere arm's length before us. That gusty morning, not four but eight new pairs of eyes glimpsed for the first time the long-sought, elusive *Betula uber.*

Some days earlier, when my poetical daughter heard that I was venturing into the southern mountains to search for a possibly extinct tree, she said: "I have visions of it deep in a great forest, draped in a golden net, with manifold birds singing on its boughs, and national foresters posted around it, holding guard dogs." However, the plant we were all gazing at was lean, birdless, and rangy—from three to five yards taller than the maximum height of twenty-five feet given by Ashe. It was crowded by similarly spindly black birches and other trees. Obviously, all of them were engaged in a struggle for sunlight on the days when this was available.

Now, looking down the creek to the north, I saw several trees with orange plastic bands tied around their trunks. These proved to be more Ashe's birches, marked by Ogle. Altogether, we counted eleven mature examples of the tree. To a casual observer, they looked much like their black birch neighbors, except for the leaves. They were comparable in height and in trunk size, and the boles of both species bore mottled gray and black bark, spotted in places with lichen. With a penknife, I cut off bits of the bark of each species. Each, I found, had a wintergreen fragrance and taste, but Ogle felt that those of Ashe's birch were somewhat the weaker. "Like teaberry gum," he said. The largest *uber* in the grove, which I measured with my pocket tape, had a circumference at breast height of about eighteen inches. I estimated it to be some forty-five years old, and Wagner said he thought that was probably close. "Birch grows slowly," he said.

Once we had identified the trees, Wagner set forth our next, equally important goal: "Have these trees been reproducing themselves? We must find that out now. We must look for seedlings." Soon our party had scattered over a wide area west of the creek. I roamed in the rain for fully half a mile, wandering over a meadow that sloped upward to the west and stopping only when I reached the border of a thick wood where seedlings would not thrive. The job was not easy for any of us. We were on Ray Haulsee's farm, with cows foraging across it. Their range included the space under the trees along the creek's west bank, and they obviously found young birch trees of any variety to their taste, for we discovered many stumps of seedlings bearing merely a leaf or two. The rain continued intermittently in hard showers and slack-offs. The cows, whose numbers seemed to increase, regarded us in a bemused fashion, their heads raised from the ground and their large eyes reflecting curiosity about the unwonted band of strangers in their midst. For our part, we regarded them with outright animosity. Everywhere, we came upon evidence of their destruction of young birches. We also came across evidence of the part of the country we were in—an empty chewing tobacco tin, a spent bottle of Dr. Pepper.

Around noon, after our four unexpected arrivals had left, our group of five drove back to Sugar Grove and ate at a lunchroom cum filling station cum general store, which served us some well-cured Virginia ham. Afterward, we drove back past the site on Cressy Creek and down the highway to the south. We branched off to the left, taking a dirt road that went up the side of a mountain. Part way up, we parked and got out to poke along its shoulders and into the woods in a survey for additional examples of Ashe's birch. Wagner was of the opinion that others might be found in the neighborhood. Ogle was not so sure. He said he had been up twenty adjacent valleys since late August without seeing any. In midafternoon, our search of the hillside having proved futile, we returned to Cressy Creek. The four botanists—Ogle, Mazzeo, Meyer, and Wagner—wanted to check the branches of the trees we had found for possible male and female catkins. Both normally occur on the same birch, and establishing their presence was necessary in order to determine whether the trees were fertile. Birch catkins combine to produce seed when wind-blown pollen from a male catkin falls on the ovary of a female catkin. The catkins start forming in late summer for the next season, the female more slowly than the male. In the spring, when both are mature, the wind does its job, and fruits are formed that contain the seeds. These seeds are inside nutlets with narrow wings, forming reproductive organs called samaras. (The best-known samara is the maple key, which is much larger than the fruit of the birch.)

The long pruner was taken from the van, and Ogle offered to climb a tree on a catkin reconnaissance. He seemed remarkably agile for a man of his size—he weighs more than 200 pounds—and quickly began making his way aloft. After several minutes of activity in the branches, he said: "I think I see something. Hand me the pruner." It was passed up to him, and Ogle, carrying the awkward instrument easily, moved still higher and out onto a branch. We heard snipping, and down fluttered cuttings. Wagner pounced on them. For some moments, he examined what he had. Then he gave an elated cry. "It's fertile! It's fertile!" Mazzeo cried: "Oh, that's marvelous! You have the male catkin, too. It's never been seen before!" Their jubilation was caused mainly by a seed or two in a decaying female catkin and some immature pollen grains in a male.

Emboldened by the knowledge that the trees could have progeny, the rest of us, under Wagner's direction, began a spirited new search for more seedlings. This time, we went to a fenced-in meadow of about an acre directly across the road to the east. It was also on Ray Haulsee's land. And there we found seedlings, from six inches to three feet high, of both the black birch and Ashe's birch. Actually, it was a logical place for them to be. The prevailing wind was from the west and would have blown seed there. As the botanists made a count of the seedlings of both species, I, at Wagner's request, stood by with paper and pencil and set down the score according to what was shouted at me by the botanists. The total was eighty-nine seedlings of *Betula lenta* and sixteen of *uber*. "That's about the same ratio found among the mature trees on the creek," Wagner declared.

It was then about five o'clock. The rain had stopped for the moment, and the sun had broken through the clouds. Ogle took us to the Ross house to meet the owner, whom he knew. The house was reached by a wide, railless plank bridge across Cressy Creek. After introductions, we were given permission to gather on the bridge for sorting and drying what seemed to me the enormous assortment of material we had collected. Ray Haulsee came over, and he, too, was introduced to us by Ogle. Both landowners were friendly men, quite interested in what we were doing. Ross took us a little way north of his house but some way south of where Ogle had found his *Betula uber*. There, close to a great pig that had earlier grunted his puzzlement at us, Ross pointed out two other examples of the birch—one mature, one a sapling—both also on the west side of the creek. This brought our total of adult specimens to twelve. When we told Haulsee about the seedlings we had found in his meadow and the damage cows had done to those on the west side of Cressy Creek, he obligingly said: "I don't have to use that field for pasture."

Our dinner that night at the motel was late. Afterward, the jungle of collected material was unloaded from the van and piled onto the covered walkway in front of the adjoining rooms of Mazzeo, Meyer, and Wagner, who, along with Ogle, diligently sorted, pressed, mounted, and labeled what seemed to me an infinitude of specimens. They worked until midnight. Next morning, I asked Ogle, who had returned to help with the uncompleted labeling, his opinion of why no *Betula uber* had been found along Dickey Creek, where Ashe had first reported it. "That's a question we'd all like to answer," he said. "I have a theory, which I'm trying to prove, that Ayres, not Ashe, found *uber*, and told his collaborator about it. Furthermore, it could be that the original trees were, in reality, found along Cressy Creek, not Dickey Creek. Ashe had a reputation in some quarters as a careless botanist, and certainly some of the data on his *uber* labels are incorrect. For example, one or two of them state that the tree was found at 3,800, not 2,800, feet. This at least lends some color to the possibility that he was wrong on other scores. However, assuming that the tree was collected by Ashe on Dickey Creek, there are several possible explanations for its disappearance from there during the last sixty years. Among these are the chance that only one or two trees existed there, and that these were competed out of existence, with no seedling survivors. I know that trees along the creek were felled for farmland. Or it is even possible that people distrusted the unfamiliar tree. Before Ray Haulsee was aware of *uber*'s botanical value, he took down, on his property, what may have been the largest member of the Cressy Creek population, because, from the shape of the leaves, he thought the tree was diseased." I pointed out that none of the full-grown *uber* we had seen seemed old enough to date back to Ayres's (or Ashe's) discovery in 1914. I said I wondered what had become of the older trees, apart from the one Haulsee had chopped down. "Right now," said Ogle, "we don't know how old an *uber* can get. One dead one I found along Cressy Creek was only nineteen years old from its rings. Better-known birch trees mature slowly. Those used for timber usually have to be 150 years old. Just what is the life expectancy of *uber* is one of the things we want to find out."

Ogle said that he and Mazzeo planned to collaborate on a scientific paper on the rediscovery of *Betula uber* on Cressy Creek, to be published in 1976, which has been done. In it he suggested that *uber* receive the common name, round-leaf birch. He also said he hoped, by some means, to get a high fence erected around the small population of trees.

Before Wagner left that afternoon, I asked him what he thought of *uber* now. "You were a doubting Thomas day before yesterday," I reminded him.

Wagner replied: "A serious botanist has to ask the questions I did. Here you have a tree that was invisible for decades following its discovery. Nobody could find it. Obviously, it was rare. Perhaps it was only a single tree. It might have been a variety created by nature—a distinctive part of a species but with different minor characteristics, such as the northern variety of the red oak, var. *borealis*, found in the colder parts of the United States. It might have been a solitary cultivar—a variety created through breeding by man but never existing in nature except as an escapee. It might have been a sterile hybrid, like a mule—a mongrel between two species of plants. Or it might have been an individual variant, a freak resulting from some genetic upset of the kind that produces the human examples seen in circus sideshows. A true species, however, has its own characteristic range on earth, its own habitat and associates. In terms of form, it has its own distinctive features, differing from those of all other species. Its individuals are more like its own race than any others. And, genetically, it is capable of creating similar offspring by fertile seeds. Although I properly came as a doubter, I now believe that *uber* has the qualifications of a true species."

Wagner said that something he planned to do at once in Michigan was to check the comparative fertility of the pollen grains from *uber* and those from *lenta,* several of whose male catkins he was also taking along. (Subsequently, he reported that *uber* seemed to be somewhat less fertile.) Mazzeo and Meyer, for their part, went back to the Sugar Grove area that afternoon to look for more *uber* and to gather more data, take more photographs, pick up more samples, and collect a few seedlings for the National Arboretum.

A few days later, in Washington, I went out to the arboretum to see whether any new developments had occurred. Mazzeo told me that while no new mature specimens had been found, Ogle had discovered five additional seedlings in Haulsee's meadow, bringing the total of these to twenty-one. Mazzeo said that considerable *uber* material had been sent to Wagner, and that one of the four seedlings brought back would also eventually go to him. The seedlings, then under the care of a competent gardener at the arboretum, were doing well, I was told. Over the years ahead, it was the arboretum's plan to grow more *uber* from seed and cuttings and, in due course, supply healthy plants to its numerous arboretum correspondents around the world, and this plan to date has been successful. Thus, even if *uber* in the wild state should ultimately die out, the plant would be preserved, as *Franklinia* has been. Today, it is the rarest birch in the country. It may be the rarest on earth, a surprising botanical vestige, seined back to human awareness by human curiosity and persistence.

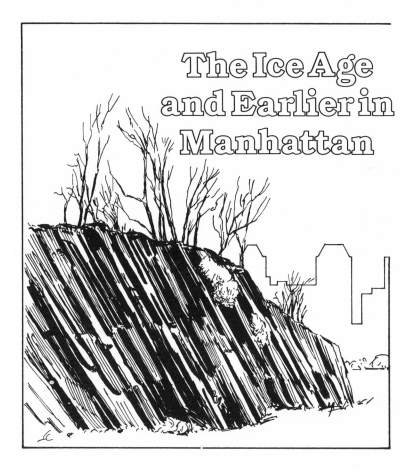

The Ice Age and Earlier in Manhattan

New York City, our nation's largest metropolis, has, in almost the center of Manhattan, the midmost of its five boroughs, the pastoral expanse of Central Park. This is, for its size, the most used park in the world. Annually more than 12 million people wander over its greensward or under its trees or take advantage in one way or another of its various lakes and streams. The 840 acres of this arm of the wild, thrust so uncharacteristically into the city's arid setting of man-made brick, macadam, and concrete, contain many products of that untamed and untamable force we call nature. Most, however, are unseen or unnoticed by the majority of park visitors.

A while back I got interested in one of these forms, the geology of the park, as evidenced by what can be seen there of the workings of nature's agencies below the surface of the earth and above it. To learn more about this, I sought out one of the experts in the area, Christopher Schuberth, for a number of years a lecturer in geology at the American Museum of Natural History in the city and an authority on the different formations of the New York City region.

"The geology of Central Park is part of that of the metropolitan area, which is one of the most diversified of any large city in the world. Within the park's square mile or so, there are boulders more than a billion years old, some of the finest examples of ice-polished rock to be found anywhere, a surface largely covered by glacially distributed rock debris, and a layer of bedrock that was formed 480 million years ago," Schuberth told me. He was chatting with me in his office in the museum a few score yards west of the park, telling me something of the park's geological history before we went out to take a look around for ourselves.

The bedrock of the park, which outcrops frequently, is, Schuberth told me, an extremely hard, durable schist—a metamorphic rock known as the Manhattan formation, the topmost of three rock units known collectively as the New York City series. It was laid down more than half a billion years ago—eons before the Atlantic Ocean existed. Where the park now lies, the earth's exterior then stood under the water of a narrow, shallow arm of the sea running into Pangaea, the huge, solitary land mass from which, by a process of separation, our present continents have been derived. To the west lay solid land of the continental interior; to the east was a chain of mostly volcanic islands; from both the arm of the sea received sedimentation through the action of weathering. Volcanic activity in the archipelago also deposited lava and ashes. The resultant sand, clay, mud, and silt, as their weight steadily increased through the millennia, sank deeper and deeper into the sea arm's floor, which by the start of the Paleozoic era some 600 million years ago had become a geosyncline—a deep flexure in the earth's crust produced by major forces operating below the planet's surface. In it the deposited material of the Manhattan formation consolidated to form a sedimentary rock known as sandy shale.

For reasons that probably had to do with movements of great terrestrial plates on either side of the sea arm, Schuberth said, the sandy shale on its floor was thrust deep into the earth. Below it, deeper down, were the other materials of the New York City series—first a whitish limestone and under it a graywacke sandstone, whose deposition had begun in late Precambrian times 700 million years ago. By the time the great downward thrust occurred, these three sediments amounted to 30,000 feet or more in thickness. Under the great pressure and high temperature of the depths, the shale that was to become the Manhattan formation metamorphosed, flowing like plastic and turning into the much harder schist—just as the application of great heat in metallurgy helps change iron into steel. As the schist cooled, its ingredients, segregated to a much greater degree than formerly, recrystallized: Quartz, feldspar, mica, garnets, and other minerals became much more visually apparent than they had been as minute particles in its sedimentary predecessor.

As the material that formed the schist was being driven down into the earth, adjoining sedimentary deposits east and west of it were forced upward following the normal course in the life of a geosyncline cycle. In response to this process, as subsidence took place in the trough, or geosyncline, the adjacent crusted areas rose as geanticlines, furnishing further sediment to the accumulation in the trough. The final phase of the cycle occurred when, in answer to further internal pressures, compressional forces operating horizontally tens of miles below the surface of the earth caused the tremendous thickness of the uplifted sedimentary strata to become folded over the geosyncline, whose deposits then became the metamorphic core of an impressive mountain system, perhaps of Himalayan stature. During the 120 million years that followed, however, erosion took its inexorable toll, and the peaks were much diminished. Then, again reacting to internal pressures caused by the need for subsurface equilibrium, masses of molten rock from the earth's interior, called magma, began forcing their way into the metamorphic base that lay beneath what is now the park. The magma intruded into the schist through narrow seams that were at most only several yards wide, but often several hundred feet in length. The magma consisted almost always of a granite pegmatite—a coarse-textured igneous rock composed mostly of massive quartz and feldspar, but bearing with it also other minerals that, upon cooling, sometimes took the form of exquisitely formed crystals, often of exceedingly large size.

The magma arrived in the park schist 360 million years ago. For the next 150 million years, erosion continued, as rain, sleet, hail, snow, and frost ate away at the craggy peaks. And as they wore down, their pressure lightened. Just as the sedimentary deposits sank as they grew heavier, so did the metamorphic core below the park rise as the weight above it decreased. Geologists agree that by 200 million years ago, when the Mesozoic era succeeded the Paleozoic, all this huge ancient mountain system had been worn away and in the area now occupied by the park the Manhattan formation schist lay exposed at the surface except at the park's extreme northern end. There, at what is now 106th Street, a fault, which is a fracture in the earth's crust where strata slide past one another, had brought to the surface the second component of the New York City series that lies just under the Manhattan formation. This is the Inwood formation, so-called from its frequent occurrence in the Inwood section of Manhattan. It is characteristically a dirty white, sugary marble, far less resistant than the schist and made from the earlier sedimentary limestone.

The three formations of the New York City series are regarded as the principal bedrock of Manhattan and the Bronx. The third and oldest rock unit, which originally had been a sandstone, is the Fordham formation, again named for its extensive emergence in the Fordham area of the Bronx. It is as hard as the schist and is an attractively banded black and white gneiss. From the Inwood formation at the park's northern end, the rock layers dip toward the south, so that at the park's middle, Schuberth told me, the Inwood marble lies hundreds of feet below the surface, the gneiss thousands of feet down. The closest gneiss to the park is east of it and south of 110th Street, where a thin strip underlies Second Avenue at some forty feet below the surface.

The history of the park's geology has some missing pages.

Early in the Triassic period, which opened the Mesozoic era, the earth's exterior in the metropolitan region, freed of the load of the old mountain system, broke into major fault sections and thrust up great blocks into another mountain system with interspersed valleys. (By this time, too, some 200 million years ago, the Atlantic Ocean was being born as a relatively slender finger of water between two parts of the now separating single land mass.) The principal relics of this newer mountain system as seen today in nearby New Jersey are the Palisades and the Watchung mountains. This was the age of the dinosaurs. Schuberth said he thought the land then resembled that found in much of our Southwest, with bare mountains and alluvial fans filling many of the adjacent valleys.

Central Park may have been a part of this system, but no evidence of it remains today. However, the fossil of a lizard, capable of flight and predating by some 20 million years the oldest flying vertebrate fossil previously discovered, was found in the rock of this formation, known as the Newark series, in North Bergen, New Jersey, just three miles west of the park, a little more than a decade ago. If the park did have Newark series material and then lost it, some of the material, Schuberth told me, was returned to Manhattan in the last century. Loads of red sandstone from the Newark series, not used or quarried any longer, were brought into the city to serve in constructing brownstone houses.

The last geological event whose record is there for us to see in the park was the work of the great ice sheet of late Pleistocene times. Some 30,000 years ago, this towering wall of ice, believed to have been more than 1,200 feet high—or as tall as the Empire State Building—slid slowly southward from Canada and covered all of what is now New York City to northern Staten Island. A glacier is the mightiest of all erosional agencies, and like most, this one removed down to bedrock much of the surface material in its path, carrying the scourings along with it. These ranged in size from vast rocks to specks of clay. Recently the annual mean temperature in the park, as measured by the instruments in the Belvedere Castle, until not long ago the city's weather observatory for the five boroughs, was a bit over fifty-four degrees Fahrenheit.

At the time of the glacier it is estimated to have been about forty. The glacier remained in place until temperatures started to rise about 13,000 years ago. Then it began gradually to melt northward, dropping on the park some of its transported load of boulders, rock, and rock debris. The retreat of the ice exposed on the park's bedrock unmistakable signs of the gigantic grinding action that had taken place under the ice's enormous weight from the stones set in the glacier's foot.

We left Schuberth's office and entered the park, perhaps fittingly, by the Naturalists' Gate at Seventy-seventh Street and Central Park West. "We'll walk northeastward through the Ramble to the Belvedere Castle, and then from there to the south of the park," Schuberth said. We crossed the West Drive, took the path over the Bank Rock Bridge, and climbed up to the Ramble, a wooded knoll of some thirty acres that lies just east of the museum. "A good deal of the Manhattan formation is visible through the park's surface," Schuberth told me. "The exposed portions are quite different in appearance from the freshly broken stone. Most outcrops are unnaturally covered with soot or grime, or naturally stained by yellow oxides of iron washed out from nearby soil. The freshly broken schist is silvery gray in color, medium- to coarse-grained, with the foliation very apparent. Commonly, flakes of the constituent Muscovite mica, named after a Russian scientist who first described it, glimmer like fish scales when exposed. Mica is a mineral silicate that readily separates into very thin leaves. Its transparent forms are called isinglass. The schist is very, very tough. It underlies practically all of Manhattan Island south of here. It gives tall buildings a firm foundation, and it has value even when excavated—the crushed, gravel-sized stone is mixed into concrete destined for heavy service."

As we walked upward, Schuberth indicated a small outcrop beside the path. "Note its smutty look, the result of decades of New York City air," he said. "And note, too, that small elm, growing from a crack, slowly, very slowly splitting this enormously hard stone, another agent of erosion." Still farther along the path, we came upon a larger, tablelike outcrop. Schuberth knelt beside it. "See the intense deformation of the strata, the lines of foliation going up and down almost like the foldings of a ribbon. Indications of similar stress would be found in the roots of the Himalayas or Alps. The foliation is turned on edge here so the mica looks like fine lines."

Shortly we reached the Belvedere. The tower of this castle-like stone building had been used first as a city and then as a federal weather observatory for more than a century. But the structure, we noticed during our walk, showed signs of the ruthless vandalism so common today throughout the park. Windows had been broken, doors forced, and great pieces of stone removed from its balustrade. Because of this destruction, the weather station has recently been forced to move to the roof of the park's precinct station house, not far from its previous site.

Even the huge outcrop it stood on, we saw, was defaced with different colored paints sprayed on from aerosol cans—another form of vandalism. Schuberth looked at this with disapproval. "It's a shame this monumental rock is so disfigured," he said.

On one shoulder of the outcrop Schuberth found a diminutive dike—a small magmatic intrusion coming up vertically through the schist. Had it been horizontal, it would have been called a sill. This dike, an almost white segment, was only an inch or two wide. However, dikes and sills up to a foot or more can be seen in the park. They are almost all pegmatites, a coarse variety of granite.

"Pegmatite dikes and sills make up less than 5 percent of the city's bedrock," said Schuberth, "so they are a distinctly minor rock type. But they are not an ordinary one." He told me that because of the great heat and pressure materials of pegmatites are subjected to as they force their way into the metamorphic rock, they often form, through the process of agglomeration of like materials that takes place under such circumstances, an unusual variety of accessory minerals when they cool—beryl, garnet, spodumene, and tourmaline, among others. And often these are produced in lovely oversized crystals. Of the 2,000 minerals known to occur on earth, some 450 are obtained from pegmatites. Of 170 or so mineral species that have been identified from the bedrock of Manhattan—a record number for an area not undergoing any kind of mining development—more than 80 percent were obtained from pegmatites. These include such unusual specimens as a ten-pound garnet crystal from Broadway and Thirty-fifth Street; a nine-inch-long, ten-pound tourmaline crystal from Fort Washington Avenue and 171st Street; and, from Riverside Drive and Ninety-third Street, one of the finest chrysoberyl crystals ever discovered in North America. Chrysoberyl, a yellowish mineral, is, like the others, sometimes used as a gem. The presence of the pegmatite-bearing schist, coupled with the numerous building and other excavations that have been undertaken in Manhattan, account for the profusion of minerals found here.

"If excavations were as common in the park as they are outside it, and if the collection of minerals were permitted, the park would doubtless have a quite impressive list of minerals found," Schuberth said. "But rockhounds are not allowed to operate in the park. Of course, small garnets can sometimes be seen in the schist itself." He pointed one out to me in the outcrop before us. Held in the rock's grubby face, it looked about the size and color of a black peppercorn.

On our way to the southern part of the park, we again passed through the Ramble. Here and there, small outcrops occurred, the dark rocks nosing through the turf. West of the band shell on the Mall, we came upon an erratic—the name for the boulders the ice sheet dropped in its retreat. This was of diabase, Schuberth said, torn from its moorings on the Palisades across the Hudson River. It is a very tough stone, essentially of triclinic feldspar, which is a mineral silicate. "During the middle of the last century, when Manhattan was growing rapidly," he told me, "this rock was quarried from the Palisades and brought to Manhattan as Belgian bluestone. It was made into cobblestones and used for street and sidewalk paving. The cobbles can still be seen on a number of downtown streets, one example being Seventh Avenue between Perry and Grove streets. Two small quarries in Rockland County still mine the stone for riprap—large pieces used in facing stretches of land to preserve it from heavy wave erosion."

We now approached what Schuberth said was one of the finest specimens of roche moutonnée he knows. The name, French for "sheep rock," comes from the rock's asymmetrical shape, which supposedly resembles that of a recumbent sheep in a field. These are outcrops over which the titanic weight of the stone-studded glacier had passed ("like a giant Brillo pad," said Schuberth). The north, or approach, face is polished smooth and bears both shallow and deep striations where abrasion has left its mark; the south, or departure, side, while polished, has no striations and is steeper, because of what Schuberth called "the plucking action of the ice." This particular roche moutonnée was a large one, near the middle of the park just east of the carousel and south of the Sixty-fifth Street Transverse Road at the level of Sixty-third Street, under the brick pavilion where now senior citizens play chess and cards. The surface was, indeed, beautifully polished as well as heavily scratched. "Observe the striations," said Schuberth, "just a shade west of north. And the gleam on the rock. Sometimes I have stood here when the sun was in the west and the rock's crust shone like a mirror."

A little farther on, we came upon another erratic north of the Sheep Meadow. It was taller than a man, and Schuberth estimated its weight at a ton or more. "This is one of the older rocks anywhere in the park. Or in the city area itself, for that matter. It's close to 1.2 billion years old. It comes from the Hudson Highlands, forty miles northwest of the city, and is a product of the Precambrian era, a bit of the core of an ancient mountain range raised in that epoch and since eroded to basement level. Part of this ancient land mass conceivably could underlie the younger metamorphic rock of the New York City formations." He told me that the Highlands complex, known as Highlands granite, contains, as does this erratic, principally mica and feldspar—the latter, like mica, a mineral silicate.

"Most of the surface of the park, under the plantings," he continued, "is glacial till. This is loose, unconsolidated material, often with complex characteristics. It overlies most of the schist. The till was dropped by the melting glacier and filled in much of the preglacial valleys, leveling out the topography, so to speak." I asked him whether it contained any fossils, since the metamorphism that created the schist would have destroyed any that had existed in previous sedimentary sandy shale, and the fiery intrusions of the dikes and sills could not, of course, have contained any. "Till outside the park has yielded fossils," he said, "including those of mastodons, which lived here in Pleistocene times. A molar tooth from one was picked up in an excavation at Broadway and Sixty-ninth Street, a block and a half from the park. Since the till around the park has fossils, doubtless there are some here, too. But fossil collecting, like mineral collecting, is forbidden in the park."

Earlier, at the museum, I had talked with Sidney Horenstein, a scientific assistant in the Department of Invertebrates, to whom suspected fossil finds on the surface of the park are generally brought for identification. "In the park, so far as we know, there have been only two, rather enigmatic fossil finds," Horenstein told me. "One was a hunk of oolitic limestone—a common building material—from Indiana. It consisted of small round grains, cemented together, and was full of tiny fossil protozoans and crinoid stems. The latter are parts of a large class of lily-shaped echinoderms, a marine animal still existing that was very common in Paleozoic times. The other was a piece of Burgess shale from British Columbia that contained trilobites, a group of now extinct marine arthropods that were numerous and common in the Paleozoic, becoming extinct at its end. In both cases the most probable explanation is that the specimens were discards from a collector's shelves. Almost nothing exists on the park's surface that could naturally contain fossils. When I take groups for walks there, I point out to them some of the erratics of igneous diabase from the Palisades, which is a nonfossil-bearing rock, of course. But I tell them that the feldspar it contains, when ground up, forms the abrasive for Ajax and other cleansers of that type."

The last geological detail Schuberth and I examined was a glacial pothole some two feet across—the only one known to exist in the park. It is not far inside the Central Park West wall at about the level of Sixty-third Street, and it was identified almost fifty years ago by an osteopath, an inveterate Central Park walker, who thought there was something unusual in the largely earth-filled depression in the flat face of the outcrop. His guess was later confirmed by one of the scientists attached to the museum's geology department, who got a digging permit from the Parks Department and reached the pothole's bottom. There, substantiating the osteopath's hunch, lay some yellow clay dating back to just after the last Ice Age. Potholes are formed when, near the front of the melting glacier, streams of water, carrying with them sand, gravel, and rock, descend to the bedrock below, usually through a deep crevasse, and form a whirlpool. The abrasives in the vortex carve out the pothole over a period of years. The pothole we saw is again largely plugged with turf.

Several natural bodies of water existed in the area before the park was laid down. Those that were retained, although somewhat altered by the park's architects, Frederick Law Olmsted and Calvert Vaux, are seen today in the interconnecting Pool, Loch, and Meer at the park's northern end; the Lake in the center; and the Pond in the southeastern corner. Originally the Pool, Loch, and Meer were a stream that rose on the park site near 107th Street near Eighth Avenue and flowed north into a pond that lay between 110th and 111th streets; the Lake is the result of a stream that entered the park site at Eighth Avenue and Seventy-fourth Street, ran a short distance into the progenitor of the Lake, and exited by going east and leaving the site at Fifth Avenue and Seventy-third Street; the Pond comes from a stream that started at Seventieth Street between Ninth and Tenth Avenues, entered the park site at West Sixty-fifth Street, crossed the area to the Pond's present spot, and exited, flowing southeasterly from Fifty-ninth Street.

To control and regulate these bodies of water today, seventy-four and a half miles of pipe have been laid in the till. Among them are a brick sewer eighteen inches in diameter running into the northeast end of the Lake to carry in runoff from the park, thus replacing the normal evaporation from the surface; a twelve-inch cast-iron pipe running from east to west to drain the Conservatory Pond where toy boats are sailed; and a fourteen-inch ceramic pipe that can be used both to lower and to raise the level of the Pond.

The park's geology has been undergoing further changes these days. Two tunnel systems have been constructed in it, one completed, the other still in progress. The smaller, completed one, which was undertaken for the New York City Transit Authority, holds subway lines running between Manhattan and Queens and consists of two parallel tunnels that enter the park's schist at Sixty-third Street and Fifth Avenue under the zoo. They separate east of the Wollman Memorial Rink, one turning south toward Sixth Avenue and Fifty-ninth Street, the other going west until it likewise proceeds south to enter Seventh Avenue at the same cross street. The last couple of hundred feet of the tunnels, surface cuts once visible to passersby, have now been filled in and the terrain restored to its former condition by July.

The second system, the largest tunnel currently under construction in the western hemisphere, is being built for the New York City Board of Water Supply. It starts from the Hillview Reservoir in Yonkers and ends across the East River in Long Island City. Work has been going on for over seven years. The huge water pipe, when completed, will be from twenty to twenty-four feet in diameter. This tunnel enters the park at Ninety-sixth Street and Eighth Avenue and crosses it southeasterly to exit under the Metropolitan Museum of Art, where it is about 700 feet down in the schist. Only about 170 feet below the museum, however, a great cavern has been carved. Plans call for it to have a base of fifty-five by seventy feet, with an arched ceiling seventy-three feet above this. Here will be installed the many valves, controls, and other machinery needed to govern the passage of water in the tunnel. The apparatus will do this remotely. Hydraulically operated mechanisms descend from the cavern. They follow a passage that drops almost 500 feet to the tunnel below. There the valves they govern regulate the water flow in the tunnel. The engineers so far have found two pegmatite dikes in the path of the tunnel under the park. Besides feldspar and quartz, the dikes contain biotite, a species of black or dark gray mica, a silicate of aluminum, iron, magnesium, and potassium—more evidence of forces that operated long, long ago in a landscape quite different from today's. The deeply concealed intrusions from the earth's fiery interior show only too clearly that then, as now, the powers of nature that fuel all animate and inanimate manifestations on this planet had long, long arms.

Wildflowers Abloom Amid the Stone

Wildness, often unrecognized, animates our countryside and suburbia. It even penetrates our cities—those jumbled piles of masonry and miles of pavement. There, in particular, it may go unheeded. But it is, nevertheless, actively present in that crowded, anomalous setting.

The examples I am most familiar with—owing to my long employment in New York City—are to be found in Central Park.

The least observant visitors there cannot fail to see the waters and the trees. But their outings are unlikely to lead them to discover the fishes and crustaceans and amphibians living in the waters. Or to find out that the trees may shelter, at various times of the year, all four species of New York state's migrating bats—the big brown, hoary, red, and silver-haired.

Still another instance of the recurring presence of nature is the park's wildflowers.

By definition, Central Park's wildflowers are those bits of bloom that, outside the formal gardens of the park, dot the tangles and the greensward. They have, alas, altered greatly in character during the more than century-long life of the park. One spring forty years ago I walked the less-frequented parts of Central Park to see what I might find in the way of the showier wildflowers, those often fragile beauties that normally grow in secluded situations and are the joy of woodland strollers at the start of the growing season. At that time, when the park's human and vehicular traffic was far less than now, I turned up four specimens. They were the adder's tongue or dogtooth violet, the jack-in-the-pulpit, the rue-anemone, and the wild geranium.

Long before that, however, a couple of decades after the park had opened in 1858 and after the vast amounts of fertile soil provided for the site had had a chance to welcome the wind-blown seeds of plant life, a writer in an 1879 issue of *Harper's Magazine* revealed that "nearly every wildflower of the field finds its congenial haunt there," thus bringing before the mind's eye in those sedate Victorian days the vision of arbutus, blood-root, columbine, hepatica, and trillium nodding in the breeze within that verdant rectangle with its handsome stone walls, created in the midst of thousands of human beings.

However, in more recent annual forays into the park over a span of years that started in 1969, I have been able to find only one of the four wildflowers I discovered forty years ago. It is the dogtooth violet, still hanging on in the park's northwest quadrant, its pendant yellow trumpet and mottled leaves erupting there from wet, marshy ground often in very early spring. Yet despite this diminution in the rarer wildflowers that once graced the park, nature has refused to be crowded out of an area whose earth still gets its allotments of sunshine and rain. During my dozens of visits within this interval of almost a decade, I have come across more than fifty kinds of wildflowers. Some of these, of course, dedicated gardeners may refer to as weeds. But they are, nevertheless, wildflowers. All except one, the Japanese knotweed, are included among the nearly 1,300 species listed in the authoritative *Field Guide to Wildflowers of Northeastern and North Central North America,* by the famed environmentalist Roger Tory Peterson and his collaborator, the late Margaret McKenny. All have blossoms of various sizes and colors.

When warmth arrived early in the year, I would start out, usually in March, to see what had poked through the ground. Besides the dogtooth violet (not a true violet at all, but a member of the lily family, whose spotted leaves resemble a snake's skin), I would almost certainly glimpse the dandelion's golden star and perhaps the small white florets of chickweed, so-called from poultry's fondness for its leaves. Somewhat later as the spring rolled on, I might find the star-of-Bethlehem, an immigrant like so many of the plants in Peterson's book and one that has a curious history. Its scientific name is *Ornithogalum umbellatum.* Botanists believe it is referred to in the Bible. In ancient Palestine, where it was extremely common, the translation of its common name was "dove's dung," doubtless because the white flowers shrouding the hillsides and open spaces made them resemble building walls that had been thoroughly blanched with bird excrement. The plant's roots, when properly treated, can be dried, ground up, and mixed with flour to make bread. The passage of 2 Kings 6:25 tells that during a famine in Samaria a measure of the plant sold for five pieces of silver.

As the spring grew older, more flowers customarily appeared, most of them lasting well into the summer or, in some cases, even into the fall. Among them was the buttercup, one of whose survival mechanisms is its acrid, stinging juice, making it unpalatable to grazing animals. Another was the cattail. Its spikes of brown flowers could be seen rising from the north end of the Pond not far from the Hotel Plaza on Fifth Avenue. Then there were the clovers, red and white (the former notable for forage and the state flower of Vermont); ground-ivy, or gill-over-the-ground, introduced to this country by early settlers and used before hops to impart a bitter taste to beer; Queen Anne's Lace, or the wild carrot, from which the garden vegetable is believed to have been derived; sorrel with its small pink flower and sour taste, much prized by the Belgians overseas for cookery; and spiderwort whose bloom is violet-tinted, the *wort* in the name coming from Middle English, where it meant "root or herb." One of my loveliest memories dates from the morning of a recent May. Crossing Burns's Lawn, a stretch of turf on the west side of the park, my companion, a Scotsman, and I came upon a carpet of azure scilla flowers that lay like a haze over the sod. My comrade said they put him in mind of shoals of bluebells in his homeland.

A surprise to me in the group of plants that blooms from springtime onward was the nightshade, *Solanum nigrum*, an inconspicuous growth quite common, it turned out, in the park. It is a cosmopolitan plant with a small, white, five-pointed flower. The plant information officer at the New York Botanical Garden told me that in this country *S. nigrum* is known as deadly nightshade. Its toxin, like that of other members of the family, is an alkaloid, found throughout the plant's structure. Studies have shown that animals ingesting its material to 0.1 percent of their weight are subject to apathy and trembling, with death occurring as the result of paralysis. Within the park it fortunately poses no threat to livestock.

Summer always brought the most flowers, some of which also lasted into the fall. Three were representatives of the thirty-odd species known in this part of the country of the genus *Aster*, so named from the starlike appearance of the flowers, the term being derived from *astēr*, the Greek word for "star." Those I found in the park bore miniblooms, mere white and yellow asterisks compared with the magnificent blue, white, and yellow luminary-like bursts that can be found almost everywhere at the ends of their stalks strewing country meadows and waste places after the summer solstice. One of the largest flowers on my list belonged to the bindweed, a vine I located on the west side of the park near the storage yard at about the level of Eighty-first Street. Its habit was to traipse through the grass and avidly climb adjacent shrubs. The blossoms resembled white morning glories. Bouncing Bet was widespread, the pink flower clusters topping a plant that seemed to do remarkably well under city conditions. Then, intermittently, I found the daisy, more formally known as the ox-eye daisy, that familiar ornament of our waysides, so fancifully styled by the poet Chaucer as "day's-eye." Perhaps the clearest blue of any bloom radiated from the dayflower. The color, in fact, seemed to have been filched from the most limpid sky of June. The plant grew low. One small white petal drooped down from the two larger blue ones. Of the many species of goldenrod that occur in the northeast section of our country, I spotted several, all rather unostentatious examples, in the park. They, like a number of the other flora noted here, belong to the family of composites (Compositae), probably the most recently evolved of the flowering plants. Yellow hawkweed with its small dandelionlike flower turned up, off and on, at this season, too.

Additional summer flowers included knotweed, both Japanese and native. The Japanese variety, despite some efforts to restrict it, had taken over much ground in the park. In July and August some areas could be almost covered with clusters of minuscule white blooms. In the park it seemed to be living up to its reputation as an aggressive weed, nearly impossible to check once established. By contrast, the native knotweed with its small pink flowers was sparsely present and inoffensive. Milkweed bearing pleasant clusters of pink or dusty rose flowers bloomed at this time of year, too, as did mullein and mustard. Both have yellow blossoms. Mullein is a lordly, rodlike plant, quite large for the park. The last one I saw stood near the western edge of the Lake, the sizable body of water near the center of the park over which one can ride in a rented rowboat. At this period, too, and often earlier, the plantain made its appearance. This is a growth common wherever there are lawns. Suburbanites detest it. Flat oval leaves circle buds tightly arranged in a center spike that resembles nothing so much as a small, green, beardless ear of wheat. The compact green arrangement is all that, at first glance, the spike seems to contain. But if one pulls it off and examines it under a hand glass usually there become visible here and there over its surface flowers like lovely, minute, white, orchidaceous trumpets often fringed with purple. Another flower that rewards closer inspection is the broad, white, flat cluster of Queen Anne's Lace. From a distance it appears to be only a wide, uniformly colored, creamy plateau. But examined more carefully, a tiny single dark floret is almost always found to lie at the center. The dazzle surrounding this makes it seem black at first, but under slight magnification it usually resolves into a rich, dark purple. Pokeweed, wormwood, and yarrow, among others, also blossom then. Pokeweed and yarrow have white flowers; wormwood, green.

The only parasite on my wildflower list was dodder, which starts blooming in July. It is a plant without leaves or green color, the body structure being long, tangled orange threads. These wrap around its hosts. Through filaments, nourishment is obtained from their tissue. Dodder's flowers are small and waxy white. This year I plucked some of the plant out of the bed of ivy before the Arsenal, the stone building near Fifth Avenue at the level of Sixty-fourth Street, which was constructed by the state in 1848. It housed soliders during the Civil War and now serves as headquarters for the Parks Department of New York City.

Among the flowers so far unmentioned that continued into the fall—some of them, when the air remained soft and mild, clear into November—were gallant soldier or galinsoga, Mexican-tea, lamb's-quarters, and smartweed. Their flowers, respectively, are white, green, green, and pink.

The largest fraction of the flowers I found was white. This is not surprising. Neither is the fact that the second largest segment was yellow. White and yellow flowers are the ones that evolved earliest in the history of the flowering plants. These started to emerge in the Cretaceous period of the Mesozoic era, which began some 135 million years ago. Today they still rule the floral landscape. Standing next on my list were the pink-to-red and blue-to-violet flowers in, as it happened, equal numbers. Very close behind them were the green flowers. There was only one brown flower, that of the cattail, and one flower that ranged from green to brown, that of the curled dock, which is one of the twelve weeds found most frequently throughout the world.

The function of flowers is to create seed, and to do that it is necessary, in almost all cases, for pollen from a stamen, the male organ of a flower, to reach a pistil, the female organ, of the same kind of flower. There the seed is formed. One of the relatively few exceptions is the dandelion. If necessary, it can produce seed without fertilization, a helpful characteristic for those of its species that bloom in very early spring before many insects, one of the two main pollinating agencies, are up and about. The other principal pollinator is the wind. Flowers that rely on it are usually dull in color and devoid of nectar and odor. They do not need these last two attributes or a bright color, which are the things that attract insects to flowers, because their blooms release vast amounts of pollen into the air. These, in the form of grains, are carried away by the wind. At least a few normally find their way to pistils of nearby plants of the same species. An example of a wind-pollinated plant on my list is the common ragweed, which has a little green flower and a bad reputation among hayfever sufferers.

The commonest insect pollinators—the honey and bumblebees, the butterflies and moths—are not frequently found in the park. Yet the wildflowers there are pollinated and cast seed. I may have found the answer last summer when I paused beside a small, pavement-bounded triangular stretch of sward a little ways from the bicycle path to the west of the zoo, a complex of buildings that lies just back of the Arsenal. There, perhaps through prior inattention on my part, I noted more insect pollinating activity than I had seen previously in the park. Smartweed, pink and white clover, gallant soldier, and lamb's-quarters were visible, and half a dozen kinds of insects were crawling or hovering over them. I observed a small wasp, two kinds of flies, a beetle, a little white butterfly that looked like a European cabbage butterfly, and a pair of tiny butterflies with rather bright but differently colored wings. Their minute appendages when extended would hardly cover a coin the size of a quarter. One of them might have been a roadside skipper, the other a male silvery blue. All the insects were attentively working the little collection of unimpressive flowers. There were even a few ants sturdily engaged in the same process.

I remember an old man in Tennessee's Appalachian mountains once saying: "There are herbs in these hills that will cure anything if you only know where to find them." In fact most of the wildflower plants on my list also have (unexpected as it may seem) tested medicinal properties. Old herbals record them at

length. And today, with the growing interest in the world of
nature, modern volumes have reprinted these qualities inherent
in plants, making them available to the organic crowd, who are
so strongly drawn just now to the uncultured products of the
earth. Of course, some of the plants have long been recognized
as therapeutic. The *United States Pharmacopoeia*, for instance,
for years has named the root of the curled dock as a gently tonic
astringent, laxative, and alterative (a medicine that gradually
changes morbid state into one of health). But much wider use
of the nonofficial agents has long been employed in, among other
places, Appalachia, where Indian and early settler customs have
persistently endured. Just a few of those in my collection used
remedially are chamomile as an insect repellant, the horse-nettle
to treat tetanus, and oil from the seed of Mexican-tea to purge
worms from animals and people. Even ragweed has a helpful
side. Its decoction has been taken for intestinal disturbances. And
the parasite dodder, too, joins the group with no less than half a
dozen roles, among them that of a fever reducer when placed in
a bath.

Cookery is a further area of considerable application for the
plants I found. Materials such as young curled dock leaves are
tasty when cooked like greens, as are the new sprouts of chickweed. These, being a little bland, are improved with the addition of sprigs of peppergrass. Lamb's-quarters, too, when prepared this way, pays large dividends in vitamins. Euell Gibbons,
the author whose books have done much to draw the attention
of interested parties to edible plants of the wild, said of boiled
lamb's-quarters: "It is a close relative of garden spinach and by
far the better plant of the two. It is richer in Vitamin C, far
richer in Vitamin A, a good source of iron and potassium, and
the richest source of calcium to be found among the leafy green
vegetables listed in the *Composition of Foods*." This is a Department of Agriculture publication. Culinary experimenters are,
however, warned against gathering their lamb's-quarters stock
from Central Park. Removal of plants or their parts from the park
is illegal. Perhaps the bitterest flavoring agent I came across was
common wormwood, only a shade less bitter than its cousin,
absinthe wormwood, the bitterest of all herbs, which I did not

find. Absinthe wormwood is the growth that flavors absinthe, the well-known, green-colored alcoholic liqueur.

The park plants have been involved with man in other ways, some serviceable, some merely odd. Bouncing Bet, the highly prized soap source of early colonists, is still recommended for washing cuts on woodland outings when soap is unavailable. The lather comes from all parts of the plant. The Romans dipped the long, dry stems of mullein in oil or suet and used them on funeral torches, referring to them as candelaria. The trefoil leaf of the red variety of clover, whose heads during the time of famine in Ireland were used as a stretcher in making bread, is one of the candidates for the original model of the shamrock, supposedly used by Saint Patrick in his teachings to illustrate the Holy Trinity and today the floral emblem of Eire. The root of goldenrod contains a yellow juice, suitable for naturally dyeing cloth, a process deemed far superior by handcrafters to the chemical method; the stalk's milky juice contains latex, from which the inventor Edison in the last century fashioned a process for producing rubber, too expensive, however, to become commercial. During World War II when kapok, the fluff of the ceiba tree of the Far East, was unobtainable, the floss of milkweed was pressed into service to stuff life jackets. Paper can be made from milkweed's stout stalks. An eccentricity connected with the dandelion will doubtless cause suburbanites to mumble: "I always knew there was something strange about that wretched plant." The dandelion exudes an ethylene gas, much like a component of coal gas, which deters other plants from growing too near it.

The wildflowers I found each year in the park were generally undersized examples of their kind. This is hardly surprising. Heavy automobile traffic rolls over the East and West drives of the park, emitting noxious exhaust fumes. And the plants have also to struggle against other city pollution that at times drifts down upon them like a toxic blanket. Also the flowers were not always the same each year. Sometimes certain species were missing, eventually to return; sometimes they did not. On the other hand, sometimes new species materialized. On the whole, the best hunting was early in the period of my recent searches. The park has deteriorated badly in the last few years—in part owing to heavy human traffic, which reaches eight figures annually, in part owing to a lack of money to hire sufficient gardening help to keep abreast of the enormous amount of maintenance needed. As a result, principally of the former factor, the space in which wildflowers can grow has continually lessened. As for the latter deficiency, I was particularly shocked on trips last year to see the widespread decay. To the east of Cherry Hill west of the Lake, for example, square rods—not yards—of earth were bare of turf and wasting away under rains. In the Ramble, the wildest part of the park, vegetation was in a neglected and sorry state, and many walkways lay in pieces and were undermined. Nevertheless, here and there across the park in sad little out-of-the-way plots and grassy scrub, I still was able to find some blooms.

The colors of thirty-six of the wildflowers I found in the park have been given so far. One species mentioned, but without giving its colors, was the ox-eye daisy. Its well-known white petals surround a golden center. For the balance, five had white flowers (the chamomile, a goldenrod, honewort, horse-nettle, and peppergrass); four had yellow ones (the beggar-ticks, butter-and-eggs, two goldenrod, purslane, and yellow clover); two had pink (the burdock and tearthumb); two had blue (the ground-ivy and loosestrife); and three had green (the clearweed, mugwort, and spurge), making in all a total of fifty-five species of wildflowers that I saw. A trained botanist during the nearly ten-year interval that I trod the park could, I suspect, have added substantially to my list. But even my amateurish efforts may surprise some in the audience as to the stubbornness of nature in inhospitable terrain.

Coyote: The Species Indestructible

Of the 4,000 species of mammals, including man, now existing in the world, 400 inhabit that part of the North American continent that lies above the border of Mexico, a tract of about 7.5 million square miles. The area comprises all of the Dominion of Canada and all the United States except Hawaii, and constitutes virtually half the land area of the Western Hemisphere. The 400 species exclude those that live in the region's inland and offshore waters —such mammals as the manatees, the seals, the porpoises, the dolphins, and the whales. One of the whales is the blue whale, which reaches a length of more than 100 feet and a weight of 125 tons, making it the largest animal of any kind to have ap-

47

peared on earth since simple chemical combinations started the upward evolution of matter on our planet that, in time, produced all forms of life, past and present. Of these life forms, mammals are the most recent and considered the most highly developed. Despite the blue whale's unique position in the hierarchy of life and the remoteness of its habitat in the far oceans, it is threatened with extinction by its fellow mammal, man, the most determined and successful predator to have evolved. Also threatened by man are many of the blue whale's smaller aquatic fellows.

Nor is man's threat confined to the water-dwelling species. As his range and numbers have increased in North America, the range and numbers of many other mammals, particularly the larger and more imposing species, have declined. Far fewer bighorn sheep and mountain goats, two of nature's surest-footed animals, leap from crag to crag on the slopes and peaks of the Rocky Mountains than was once the case. The huge buffalo herds that roamed our plains barely a century ago have vanished forever. Such a sizable predator as the grizzly bear is also dwindling in number.

Among the larger land mammals listed by our federal government as endangered or threatened with extinction are the eastern cougar, the Sonoran pronghorn antelope, the grizzly bear, and, in the lower forty-eight states, both species of resident wolf, the red wolf and the timber wolf. The Defenders of Wildlife, a conservationist organization based in Washington, D.C., would add to this list at least five others—the wolverine, the fisher, the bobcat, the lynx, and the bighorn sheep. Among the larger aquatic species the federal government lists as endangered or threatened are eight species of whales, including the blue whale, and the manatee. Defenders of Wildlife would add one other—the river otter. Whatever the actual count of species in trouble north of Mexico, it seems unquestionable that the number of mammals there is far less today than several hundred years ago.

To be sure, not every one of the area's mammals is, at the moment, in full retreat before man. Some, including as large a species as the white-tailed deer, have, particularly of late, managed a modus vivendi with him. A handful of others, including the opossum and the armadillo, strange and rather lowly forms of mammals, have actually increased their range. The opossum is a marsupial, the female carrying her young in a pouch on her belly. The armadillo is almost toothless and covered on body, tail, legs, and top of head with small bony plates of armor. When it wants to cross a stream, it holds its breath and walks over the bottom. The two are descendants of ancient refugees from South America, where they developed when that continent was an island 20 million years ago. Many unusual forms of life were produced in the isolation of that evolutionary backwater, although most of those that were spectacularly different succumbed to the more efficient mammaliain species that later moved in from the north following the rise, several million years ago, of the Panama Portal, the land connection that joined North and South America, eventually forming the New World as we know it today. But the opossum and the armadillo did not disappear. Instead, over the millenniums, they inched their way northward until at present they are increasing their range and numbers in a modest way in many of the lower forty-eight states.

However, by any criterion the most dramatic exception by far to the general rule that animal range and numbers shrink before man has been the coyote, less commonly known as the prairie, the brush, or the little wolf. There may, of course, be some increases in the numbers of rats and mice, but these mammals are hardly wild. They are camp followers of man and the beneficiaries of his spread. The coyote, by contrast, a creature unquestionably wild, has recently staged an expansion in range and abundance that is nothing short of remarkable. Much of the expansion has occurred in this century, when man's pressure on all forms of wildlife has been at an all-time high. Part of the pressure has been a steady rise in man's occupation of wildlife habitat, including that of the coyote. And in the coyote's original homeland in the West, the pressure has included the most intensive persecution ever known to have been visited on any animal in this country or, in all likelihood, the world. The campaign, decades long, was started in the last cenurty and was aimed at nothing less than the extermination of the species. The overall procedure, which still continues, is hard to match for cold fury. However, not only has the coyote frustrated this long attempt at eradication, keeping its population more or less stable even on the battlefield, but the breed has had the vigor, as well as the intelligence, to radiate outward.

The Indian aborigines of North America for centuries lived in harmony with nature in what might be described as an ecological honeymoon. They killed for food. Even as they did so, many breathed a prayer to the dying animal, in effect asking its pardon. The Zuni hunter killing the deer, said: "Thanks, my father. This day I have drunken your sacred wine of life." On the ground he left bits of the quarry as tokens to propitiate nature and the rest of wildlife.

The white man who set foot in the New World lacked this philosophy. He lived almost without exception in *dis*harmony with nature. Instead, he worshipped inventions, material goods, and technical skills. His descendants, now mounting into the hundreds of millions, feel much the same today. But few of them display the kind of extreme reaction so common to the hardened coyote detester. In general, these people feel outraged, baffled, and half-defeated by the breed. A western sheepman not long ago violently attacked a dead coyote, kicking the carcass with one foot and then the other. "The goddamned lion is not the king of beasts," he roared. "The goddamned coyote is." Considering the animal's intelligence, adaptability, prudence, hardiness, and fecundity, there may be some truth in the stockman's statement.

When the white man first entered the New World, the coyote was found only in the West. East of the Mississippi River it was absent. Its stronghold was the grassy plain that extended from what is now southern Saskatchewan and Manitoba through the large western states that lie below them. It was also found in what is presently our Southwest and in similar terrain, both grassy and arid, in Mexico. Large predators—cougars, bears, and wolves—that occupied the surrounding forested areas prevented it from leaving its open habitat. These larger animals preyed on the coyote and kept it confined.

Today, however, despite persecution and man's territorial pressure, the coyote has been reported from every state in the Union except Hawaii, and from every territory and province of the Dominion of Canada except Prince Edward Island and Newfoundland, insular components of our neighbor to the north. And Prince Edward Island may not lack coyotes for long. Only nine miles separate it from the nearest point on the mainland, and in winter pack ice overlays the water for months, forming an excellent coyote highroad.

The North American continent has five biomes. These are biological communities characterized by distinct types of vegetation that thrive in the climatic conditions of the region. To the two biomes originally occupied by the coyote—the grasslands and the desert—have been added the tundra, the coniferous forest, and the deciduous forest. With man's virtual elimination of its animal enemies—the cougar, the bear, and the wolf—the coyote has been free to break out of its original preserve and has steadily and unhesitatingly done so. Its territory now reaches from Panama to the Arctic Ocean, a distance of more than 5,000 miles, an area greater than that occupied by any other land mammal in the world. The outraged sheepman may have had a point.

The correct pronunciation of coyote is generally considered to be "*ky*-oat." However, the closer one gets to the Mexican border the more one is apt to hear the alternative "ky-*oat*-ee." The uninformed eastern pronunciation, "*coy*-oat," is strictly bush.

The word comes into English straight from the Spanish conquistadors, who took the name for the animal, *coyotl*, from Nahuatl, the language of the Aztecs, and changed it to "coyote." The Aztecs, the last Indian rulers of Mexico, and the Toltecs, who ruled for half a millennium before them, both had a high regard for the coyote. They incorporated its form into their architecture, sculpture, and written records, and onto their battle shields. In the city of Teotihuacán, the largest and most impressive ceremonial site yet uncovered in pre-Columbian America, is a frieze of the animal in the Temple of Quetzalcoatl, the chief deity of the Toltec pantheon, whom the Aztecs united with their own war god, Huitzilopochtli. Quetzalcoatl is the white god who, according to legend, journeyed to the Gulf of Mexico and sailed away to the east, promising some day to return. When Cortés and his soldiers landed, the Spanish leader was mistaken by the Aztecs for Quetzalcoatl, a misjudgment that aided considerably in his conquest. Some elite Aztec warrior groups had long put themselves under the protection of the coyote. Although the precise reasons for this may never be known because of the wholesale destruction of Aztec records by the Spanish, the assumption is that the Aztecs felt the coyote possessed magical powers, a belief that persists in some parts of Mexico today.

The coyote was known to man long before it was known to the ancient peoples of Mexico. Exactly when prehistoric man, who is believed to have been principally of Mongoloid stock with some admixture of Ainu and Caucasoid elements, entered the North American continent by way of the Bering land bridge from northeast Asia is presently a matter of academic dispute. But whether the date was 30,000 years ago, 50,000 or, as some scholars calculate, 100,000 years ago, when man reached the North American grasslands he found the coyote already there.

The coyote is the only one of the eight living species of *Canis*, the genus, or biological grouping, of dogs, that is completely North American. Its origins were here and it has never gone elsewhere. That cannot be said of other *Canis* species. All three jackals—the golden, the black-backed, and the side-striped —are of Old World distribution; the dingo belongs to Australia; and the two recognized full species of wolves—the red wolf and the timber wolf—both now found in this country, are believed to have originated in Eurasia and to have taken up a permanent abode in North America at some presently unspecifiable time in the past. As to the last member of the genus, the domestic dog, the time of its arrival here seems somewhat clearer. Its earlier history, though, is foggy. A fossil found at Quercy, France, Cynodictus by name, dating back between 60 million and 40 million years ago, is considered by most paleontologists to be the earliest known ancestor of the dog. Cynodictus's descendants, along with the forerunners of the two species of wolves, are believed to have wandered for enormous periods of time across Europe and Asia and into North America, and then out again, in a continual search for better living conditions. These journeyings were not peculiar to the canids. Many other animals of the time also had no fixed habitat. The pathway into North America could have been from either the east or the west. The Bering land bridge rose and sank sporadically over the past 60 million years. Europe and North America were also joined for the first part of that interval, their final separation taking place at the north about 50 million years ago. Notwithstanding the uncertain date at which the wolves may have located here, it appears self-evident that the original domesticated dog, whatever may have been its form (and this could have been quite varied), came to the continent with the first human arrivals. Today's many races of the dog are purely the result of centuries of selective breeding by man.

Meanwhile, the coyote evolved in North America and stayed put. Its fossils can be found throughout the western United States from Nebraska and Texas to California. The oldest ancestor thus far unearthed, dating back 9 million years, is *Canis davisi*. What scientists describe as a "good" coyote, 3 million years old, *Canis lepophagus*, sharing morphological features with today's animal, was found in Cita Canyon, Randolph County, Texas, and described in 1938. When *Homo sapiens*, or his immediate predecessors, reached the temperate open country of North America, the coyote was there to greet him—and, if possible, of course, to steal from his larder.

As the ancestors of the Indians spread in all directions across the continent, developing into the numerous tribes that were present when the white man came, those that inhabited the coyote region developed a close association with the animal. In general, it was greatly respected and in many cases revered. In some tribes it was a figure of central importance in the creation myths, a manitou figure. The Crow Indians regarded the coyote as the supreme worker, the creator of the world, its inhabitants, and all human customs. To the Navajos, it was one of the first powers to emerge from the darkness at the beginning of things. The Flathead Indians called it the most powerful and favorable to man of the unseen forces of nature. But even those who respected and revered it saw another side to the coyote— the trickster. They watched it, for example, in company with a badger as the badger dug swiftly into a gopher hole. The coyote meanwhile stationed itself at the burrow's exit hole. When the fleeing gopher popped out, the coyote gobbled it up. Some Indians viewed the coyote as the representation of mischief and the more uncontrollable aspects of sex. The Apaches put this rather neatly. They said that in prehuman times the coyote created a path that man was foredoomed to follow—a path of gluttony, falsehood, dishonesty, lust, and other weaknesses. "Coyote did first what man does now," the Apaches said. "We are still following coyote."

In the seventeenth century, when Spanish explorers visited our plains, they saw around the Indian villages semidomesticated animals somewhat resembling coyotes. These were used as beasts of burden. Whether the villagers took the coyotes with them when they moved, or trained others at the next stop, is not known. The Indians served the young of these animals to their white guests as a special treat.

The scientific name of the coyote, *Canis latrans*, was given by Thomas Say, the scientist who first described the animal in 1823. The name means "barking dog," which is really a rather inadequate term considering the variety of sounds a coyote can make. The type specimen was taken by Say, a zoologist attached to the Long Expedition to the Rocky Mountains, which was under the command of an army officer of that name. The expedition left Pittsburgh, Pennsylvania, in 1819 and returned a year later. The type specimen was obtained near the west bank of the Missouri River in Washington County, Nebraska, about a dozen miles southeast of the present town of Blair. A type specimen, if preserved, is the model to which all future specimens are referred when morphological details are in question. However, as is the case with many early American type specimens, that of Say's coyote has disappeared. Beginning with the last decade or so of the nineteenth century, the preservation of type specimens has improved. They usually consist of the animal's skeleton and skin or, more generally, the skull and skin. Numerous type specimens of coyote subspecies taken more recently are in museums around the country.

Man has observed the coyote so closely for so many years that much is known about it. It seems to display almost the same amount of variation as do human beings. It can be brave or cowardly, cautious or rash, lazy or enterprising, physically weak or physically strong, alert or dull. In size and weight, too, it may deviate considerably from the norm at either end of the scale. Despite the intensity with which man has studied it for so many years, the coyote is still capable of producing surprises, however. Those most familiar with the animal would be the first to say that much about it remains mysterious.

The average adult male coyote rather resembles a tall, skinny German shepherd dog. It stands between twenty-four to twenty-six inches high at the shoulder, weighs from twenty to fifty pounds, and is from three and a half to four and a half feet long, including a twelve- to sixteen-inch-long bushy tail. It carries this tail, not high as a wolf does, but low, sometimes between its hindlegs. The average adult female is four-fifths the male's size. The largest coyote yet recorded was a male measuring five and a quarter feet long and weighing almost seventy-five pounds. It was taken some years back in Wyoming. Like all members of the dog genus, the species has an anal gland that becomes active when another canid approaches and sniffs. The scent is peculiar to that animal and no other. Presumably also carried in the urine, the scent is used in territorial marking. In all likelihood, this custom of marking permits coyotes to have an accurate sense of their neighbors.

The coyote's outer fur is long, rough, and grayish, growing darker on the back. It covers a soft and comparatively short underfur. Legs, paws, muzzle, and back of the ears are more yellowish in color than the upper part of the body, and the throat and belly are lighter still. The tail is darker on top than below. Coyotes of the southern deserts, blending with their surroundings, tend to be paler in tone than those of more northerly regions. The feet and belly parts of some of the more extreme southern forms are sometimes almost devoid of hair. Individuals in the northeastern part of this country appear to be a darker and somewhat heavier strain than the average. Albinos also occasionally occur. The molt is once annually, a lengthy process usually starting in early summer and completed in early fall.

The coyote's canine teeth are large for its size, being an inch and a half in length. The neck is unduly thick and heavy in proportion to the body, allowing the animal to deliver a strong bite. It can do this in a flash. A federal Fish and Wildlife representative in the West told me: "The speed of their bite is amazing. No matter what care I use in handling one, I can't always escape its bite." If the teeth get a good hold, the bite has a shearing-tearing effect, the shearing done by the knife-edged molars and the tearing by the canines.

The eyes are yellowish with black pupils and somewhat slanted, giving the coyote a rather wily appearance, which perhaps it deserves. The vision these wily-looking eyes afford is deemed equal to that of the greyhound. The large pointed ears, facing forward but very mobile, are excellent for picking up faint sounds such as those made by mice moving under snow, creatures the coyote hunts in winter. Judging from its tracking actions, the coyote's nose seems as reliable and sensitive as that of the most accomplished hound. In fact, its senses of hearing and smell are so keen that if a coyote sounds an alarm, other coyotes can change direction in midstep, a remarkable show of agility that may be without parallel in the animal kingdom. The muzzle is almost in a straight line with the forehead, giving the animal a nearly Grecian nose.

Man is the only North American mammal more vocal than the coyote. The coyote's evening serenade is a famous feature of the West. Hearing it for the first time is an unforgettable experience. An outdoorsman who listened to it once again while lying in a sleeping bag on a recent frosty, moonlit night in Alaska said: "It's spooky. The hair on your neck rises. You go back in time a long, long way." Unlike a dog or a wolf, whose howls begin low and mount gradually in pitch and volume, a coyote's howl starts with a high, sharp "yip, yip, yip" and slowly falls to a sad, haunting diminuendo. But this is by no means its only sound. It has a host of others—barks, squeaks, squeals, wails, growls, and an entire series of brief signals to its young. A recognized authority on the coyote believes an analytical study of recordings of its langauge would be as rewarding as those done recently on bat and porpoise calls.

Coyote longevity depends largely on intelligence and luck. Most deaths occur among the young. Birth to two years of age is the most critical time. A study of more than 100 carcasses collected from trappers from January through early April of a recent year showed 45 percent of those taken to be less than one year old and another 35 percent to be less than two years old. Over long periods of time, biologists feel, the birth rate and death rate balance out. Periods of abundant food allow the population to increase. The reverse provokes decline. A coyote in the wild past two years of age can, with luck, reach an age of ten years or more. A female taken on the range in Colorado was more than fourteen years old. The age of wild coyotes can now be told by a dentition technique. A tooth is sliced and a section stained. This allows the annual growth rings, like those of a tree, to be counted. Coyotes held captive in zoos have, as might be expected, longer life spans than their wild cousins. One kept at the National Zoological Park in Washington, D.C., early in this century was more than eighteen years old when it died.

A healthy coyote is a hard pack of bone and muscle. Its endurance is remarkable. It can gallop easily for long stretches of time at twenty-five miles an hour. Top speed is usually given at forty-three miles an hour, a figure that places the coyote among the fleeter species. A cheetah, the fastest land animal, is credited with seventy miles an hour. A pronghorn antelope reaches sixty-one; a charging lion, fifty. However, like all quadrupeds, some coyotes can run faster than others. One in Texas was clocked by the driver of an automobile for half a mile at fifty-five miles an hour. The coyote is also an able swimmer. One was seen crossing without difficulty a swift, canyon-walled section of the Rio Grande where it is 100 yards wide. The coyote can swim under water as well. One dived into a lake after a duck. The duck submerged. So did the coyote. After a while the coyote came up with the duck in its mouth and climbed the bank. It was then shot. The duck was found to have been bitten in the head. Despite such feats, the coyote is far from a water worshipper. But water is, of course, essential to it, as to all animals. In deserts and arid terrain where water is absent on the surface, the coyote digs for it. His nose tells him where. He goes after it by excavating a hole, but a hole on a slant so that the water, when found, is protected from the sun—a typical example of coyote smarts. The paws with which the coyote digs are longer and thinner than those of a dog the same size. The claws, blunted from continual contact with the ground, are not used in attack or defense.

What the coyote puts into its stomach intentionally, either in whole or in part, is as diverse as, if somewhat different from, the comprehensive contents of Fanny Farmer's *Boston Cooking-School Cookbook*. More omnivorous than hog or man is one description of the animal. Among items taken from its alimentary tract over the years have been rawhide ropes, string, paper, cloth, automobile tire rubber, harness buckles, horned toads, frogs, mice, rats, gophers; gobbets of bobcat, house cat, skunk, armadillo, peccary, grizzly bear, sheep, deer, elk, beaver, porcupine, and coyote; turtles, crayfish, snails, beetles, grasshoppers, crickets, ants, centipedes, bumblebees, and flies; wild berries, grapes, dates, peaches, prunes, carrots, sweet peppers, tomatoes, watermelons, plums, pumpkins, oranges, tangerines, apples, acorns, pears, figs, apricots, cherries, cantaloupe, pine nuts, peanuts, green corn, and grass. Food categories whose components are too abundant to enumerate are many kinds of fishes, birds' eggs, waterfowl, land birds (including the turkey vulture), snakes (including the bull snake and rattlesnake), honey, bread, and sugar. Apart from these dainties, the coyote has, of course, its dietary staples. These are chiefly rabbits, other rodents, and carrion. During this century in the West the contents of tens of thousands of coyote stomachs have been analyzed by federal biologists. One of the larger studies, done on nearly 15,000 stomachs over a five-year period in seventeen states, showed rabbits to constitute 43 percent of the diet and rodents, mostly mice and ground squirrels, 33 percent. Poultry, game and nongame birds, livestock, big game animals and vegetable matter made up the rest of the fare. The traces of livestock found in the stomachs were mainly sheep and goats; those of big game animals chiefly antelope, deer, elk, bighorn sheep, and bear. It is not known what proportion of these was carrion. Observation suggests that the coyote eats far more carrion in winter than at other times of the year.

To obtain food, the coyote, if left alone by man, often uses a particular hunting route for its entire life. The route may be composed of game, cattle, or sheep trails interspersed with old woods roads, dry washes, swamps, and ditch banks. Sometimes one of the sections, for example, a woods road, may be favored as a hub from which the coyote branches out on expeditions to either side. In good game country, the hunting route, usually comprising ten miles or less, may lie within a fraction of a square mile. The important thing is that it provide enough food. An optimum of 1.3 pounds and a minimum of 0.9 pound of meat, according to one authority, is what an active coyote needs daily. This translates, for example, into 75 jackrabbits or 5,000 mice annually. In addition, some nonanimal food—insects, fruit, and other vegetable matter—is normally consumed. Many individual hunting trails overlap, as the coyote seems to make no defense of territory except during the denning season. The territorial sense of coyotes is, in fact, still a cloudy area. When game declines, the animal must enlarge its circuit. Large feeding territories of more than twenty square miles have been checked by radio tagging of individuals. More often than not, the coyote hunts alone. But pairs or larger groups have been known to work in relays to run down swift prey like jackrabbits or antelope. A hunting combination frequently seen is coyote and badger. They may help one another in digging out a gopher. But usually the coyote lets the badger do the digging. Man has noted this association for ages. A clay pot made 1,000 years ago by the Indians of northern Mexico shows a badger's head on one side and a coyote's on the other. The Aztec name for badger was *tlal-coyotl,* or "earth coyote"—the coyote in other words that lives, or digs, in the ground.

Although man is the coyote's greatest enemy, it has others.

The one it fears most is the cougar, or mountain lion. Although a grizzly bear or a wolf will kill a coyote if it can, should either of these predators down a quarry, eat its fill, and depart, the coyote will close in and devour what's left. Not so with a carcass that the coyote's nose tells it was the work of a cougar. Even though the carcass is deserted, the coyote will give it a wide berth lest the cougar make a stealthy return. In a quick rush the big cat could seize the scavenging coyote before it could flee.

The pattern of coyote life is nothing like the complicated hierarchy of the wolf pack with its rigid ranking system. Coyote society centers around a reproductive female and her mate. Sometimes one or more unattached coyotes, grown offspring sometimes and sometimes nonrelatives, join the couple for companionship or hunting benefits. Whether coyotes mate for life, as wolves do, has not yet been determined with certainty. Some seem to, others not. In any event, a pair bond must be formed between a male and a fertile female as a necessary preliminary to the successful raising of a litter and the perpetuation of the species. With a permanently mated pair, the bond is already present. Otherwise it is formed when the female, coming into heat in midwinter, emits a sex attractant. Biologists are presently unsure exactly what causes the onset of estrus, but it may be the lengthening daylight. Unattached males follow the female. Like at least one other well-known mammalian species, the female picks her mate from the train of suitors. As she grows heavy with young, she and the male normally move into a den, which may be one they have occupied previously, a new site they excavate, or a vacant badger or rabbit burrow they enlarge. Sometimes more than one den is prepared. Less frequently, whelping takes place above ground in a hollow log or under a thicket. Often an infertile female, daughter or unrelated, joins the pair, acting as babysitter. Not all female coyotes come into heat. When game is scarce, perhaps only half do, nature acting in this way to avoid a population disaster. Nor are male coyotes, like dogs, sexually active year round. Their sexual activity is restricted to the several cold months when the females will permit copulation. Thereafter, their energy is expended on pup rearing and coping with the normal hazards of coyote life.

The young, born in early spring after a two-month gestation period, are toothless, blind, essentially hairless, and completely helpless. They weigh about half a pound. Five to seven make up an average litter, although the female has eight to ten nipples. However, far larger litters are on record. Some of fourteen are reliably known, and at least one of nineteen has been reported. Several authorities, however, question the figure, believing the pups to be the product of two females. They cite the virtual impossibility of one dam caring for so many young. (The largest litter of puppies known to the American Kennel Club is sixteen, but in this case man could aid in the upbringing.) The female coyote before birth often pulls fur from her belly, baring the nipples; the fur is used for bedding.

The pups feed on milk for the first ten days of their lives. By then their fur has appeared and their eyes have opened, allowing them to move around somewhat, an ability that increases each day. Before six weeks, they can run. By three weeks the full set of milk teeth arrives. Milk is then supplemented by regurgitated food, offered by both parents. By the time the pups can run, they are fed mice, which their teeth can then handle; soon the mouse diet is augmented by larger pieces of food. From midspring to early summer the pups leave the den with their parents for training. Freezing, hiding, and following are taught by the parents' vocal commands. Obedience to these increases the pups' chances of survival during the period when the family leaves the den for good, in late June or July. The group then wanders about as a unit. Sometime between August and November the family breaks up. The adults may stay together, in which case one or more of the pups may join them. Or the adults may part and the whole family scatter. By December, their ninth or tenth month, the young are at full adult size and weight.

The male throughout the reproductive period is an admirable parent. He helps excavate, and he alone guards, the den. Both before and after parturition he fetches food for his mate, who when nursing needs nearly a pound of meat daily. He feeds the pups regurgitated food and actively assists in their schooling. Without his contributions, the family could not be raised. Although the coyote normally runs from man, a federal Fish and Wildlife official told me that more than once when he was riding horseback near a den the male coyote rushed at him in a challenging way. The male coyote regularly plays with his pups. Play by an adult animal, zoologists believe, is a mark of intelligence.

Intelligence is indeed the mark of the coyote that survives. Observers over the years have noted ample evidence of this. A coyote crossing an automobile highway has been seen to look both ways. A coyote-proof fence does not exist. Using its claws to get a grip, the animal easily climbs a high wire fence. The Friends of Animals, a conservationist organization based in New York, records that one coyote scaled a fine-wire-mesh fence twenty feet high. "Up and over," said Cleveland Amory, the president. The Guatemalan Indians say: "The coyote speaks to the fence and the fence lets him through." Coyotes have also learned to utilize fences in catching game. Working as a team, they drive a swift deer or a pronghorn antelope against the fence and corral it. Two coyotes can safely kill a porcupine. Keeping out of the way of its flashing quill-filled tail, they put their paws under the animal, roll it over, and expose its unprotected belly. A captive coyote knew to the fraction of an inch the reach of its twenty-foot chain. Woe to the mouse that ventured too near. Another captive, by furiously stamping with its forepaws and then rolling on the flames, extinguished small fires set intentionally by the outdoorsman who owned it. "All coyotes put out fires," he asserted.

One wild female apparently possessed a sense of numbers. She was seen for more than an hour to search for her ninth pup, while its eight small siblings trailed in puzzlement after her. Pursued by hounds, a coyote leaped on a moving freight-train flatcar and rode triumphantly to safety. In Texas late last century, when chickens sometimes roosted in trees, coyotes on moonlit nights would dizzy the fowls by whirling round and round the trunk until a chicken dropped into thier jaws. They watch a buzzard's flight to locate carrion. In snow coyotes walk behind elk, whose hoofs turn up mice. They have been known to try and lure a hunter away from a wounded fellow coyote. One coyote, caught by the leg in a steel trap with a chain to which a three-pronged grapple hook was attached, attempted to walk dragging the trap. He was impeded by the hook, which kept catching in the ground. Finally the coyote picked up the hook in its mouth and proceeded to move forward more briskly, having solved that particular problem.

From the beginning of the sheepherding industry in the American West, a little more than a century ago, its history and that of the coyote have been closely intertwined. But the history of domesticated sheep goes back much farther. Husbandry of sheep is one of the oldest, as well as one of the most important, agricultural enterprises in the world. Sheep were first domesticated in the Old World about 7,000 years ago. They are mentioned often in the Bible. The ancient Hebrews were simple shepherds. One such was the patriarch Abraham, founder of Judaism and revered by Christians and Moslems as well. Some 4,000 years ago when he wandered across Mesopotamia on his way to Canaan (today's Republic of Israel and nearby Arab territory), a variegated flock, largely of sheep, straggled along with him. In the flock was one black goat to about every ten sheep. For a while, sheepherders in our own West experimented with this Biblical precedent, keeping one black sheep for every hundred white, which made it easier to count the number in a flock.

All the many breeds of domestic sheep—and there are more than a score—are believed to be descended from just two species of wild sheep, the urial of southern Asia and the mouflon of Europe. The mouflon ancestors are thought to have lived in the mountains of Greece and adjacent islands. Wild urials still inhabit the mountains of northern India, and the mouflon may be found today in the more desolate uplands of Sardinia and Corsica.

Wild sheep are high-spirited, daring, and self-reliant. Although the rams, and sometimes the ewes as well, often possess formidable horns, the animals' main protection is their bleak and inhospitable habitat. Living in bands, they range rugged plateaus and high mountains. The fiercest winter storms do not disturb them. They climb to loftier heights than any other animal except the goat. However, over the centuries man, with studied determination, has selectively bred for sheep that are dispirited, undaring, irresolute, and without horns. Docility is a characteristic that permits large flocks to be managed much more easily. But in the breeding process man has made the sheep the most helpless and defenseless of all livestock.

Prehistoric man domesticated the sheep for its hide and milk. Much, much later its wool became important. Although lamb and mutton are among the most palatable and nutritious of meats, not until a mere 200 years ago did breeders turn their attention seriously to developing sheep as meat animals. Now most of the sheep in our West are raised for this purpose. Although its milk, one of the sheep's original attractions for man, has more protein and mineral content than cow's milk, being on a par with the rich milk of the goat, it is largely disregarded in this country because the breeds we prefer do not produce enough of it. But heavy-milking sheep are raised in Germany and Israel. The milk there is turned into yogurt and cheese. The best-known cheese from sheep's milk is the French-made Roquefort, whose gusty, acrid flavor enjoys a worldwide reputation. In this country what we derive from the sheep is limited to wool, leather, lamb, and mutton. Also, we produce a raft of cosmetics and ointments made with lanolin, the purified fat or grease from the sheep's fresh fleece.

If we omit the sheep carried to Greenland by the Norse in their abortive attempt to settle that island and those that later accompanied Norsemen to Vinland, which may well have been a northeastern section of North America, the first sheep that entered the Western Hemisphere were brought by Christopher Columbus. Knowing what was on the other side of the world and how to get there, Columbus on his second voyage carried sheep. The first were set ashore on the present island of Santo Domingo in November 1493. The next month more were landed in Cuba.

The first sheep to arrive in the original thirteen colonies were brought to Jamestown in Virginia in 1607, but were eaten during a famine that winter. More were imported two years later, with poor reproductive results. Reproduction improved slightly with the introduction of another batch in 1611. In 1624 Massachusetts got its first sheep, as did, a year later, the Dutch colony of New Amsterdam, later to become New York. During the next 200 years, the husbandry of sheep, whose main use was to provide wool for clothes, expanded throughout the northern colonies. The pursuit was less important in the South, where people had cotton for clothes. Virginians, like most southerners, generally possessed only mediocre sheep. An exception was George Washington. At Mount Vernon during the six years that followed the end of the Revolution, he improved his flock to the extent that he felt it was producing at its maximum potential. His correspondence shows he wished to do even better by importing new breeds, but this ambition had to be laid aside with his accession to the presidency.

In Virginia, as elsewhere, the greatest obstacles to sheep raising were wolves and dogs. Citizens of this period in Connecticut and Massachusetts were so outraged by these predators that they passed laws requiring that dogs that bit or killed sheep be hanged. Executions were usually carried out in swamps. A common place name in colonial Connecticut and Massachusetts was Hang-Dog Swamp. During the eighteenth century, islands like Nantucket and Martha's Vineyard became vast sheep havens because wolves had been exterminated there. However, for most of the years before and after the Revolution the leading sheep area in the East was Vermont.

Both the Revolution and the War of 1812 sharply increased the demand for local wool. Imports were unavailable and the need for wool for uniforms was acute. After 1812, sheep raising began slowly to move westward. Pennsylvania, Ohio, Michigan, and eventually Illinois pastured sheep. The growth of cities and the increased use of machinery capable of making wool cloth more quickly stimulated the industry, as did the growing urban appetite for mutton and lamb. As a consequence, the meat of sheep began to rival wool in importance in the minds of the herders. On the eve of the Civil War, sheep raising was on the verge of moving west of the Mississippi River, a step that would plunge it into the heart of coyote country. Soon after hostilities ceased, the move was made.

By 1870, a line of thinly settled states, still largely in the pioneer stage, lay just west of the Mississippi River. Beyond them, ranging westward to the Pacific slope, the land was buffalo and Indian country. This territory stretched from the Red River, now separating Texas and Oklahoma, to the Red River of the North, marking the present Minnesota–North Dakota boundary. The vast expanse totaled better than 1 million square miles, virtually all of it in the public domain. Sheepherders about this date began appearing in large numbers, attracted by the free grazing available throughout the year. Their only expenses were for labor and supplies, their initial outlay merely the cost of the sheep and a camp outfit. By 1884 the area had become so productive of sheep that there were better than 50.5 million animals, exclusive of lambs, in the country, an all-time record.

Naturally the herders fought the coyotes. Beginning in 1860 and continuing until 1885, in much of the region an intensive campaign of poisoning was conducted by professional agents, none of whom probably had ever heard of the balance of nature or would have cared if they had. They sedulously baited the carcasses of buffalo, antelope, deer, elk, and birds with strychnine, a traditional rat poison obtained from the seeds of a tree native to India. The toll of wildlife was tremendous. The agents' aim was to collect the bounties paid for dead wolves and coyotes, but during the lengthy operation hundreds of thousands of other flesh-eating animals—bears, cougars, badgers, bobcats, kit foxes, and prairie skunks among others—perished also. The poisoners were only trying to make big business out of what had long been official policy toward the coyote in the West. The example, in 1825, only two years after Thomas Say had described the coyote, the young state of Missouri placed a bounty on it.

According to today's conversationists, the professional poisoners were ecological cretins. Nonetheless, poisoning of the coyote continues in the West, including the vast domain of public lands. However, the situation at present is quite different from that in the nineteenth century when vast quantities of wildlife were egregiously slaughtered, often mindlessly and always without protest. Now the country has numerous conservation organizations whose energetic members use legal means to prohibit maltreatment of wildlife and educational programs to argue that there is no such thing as a bad animal. This puts them directly at loggerheads with the sheepmen, who believe wholeheartedly that the coyote is a bad animal—a very bad one. Natural enemies, these two factions face one another without compromise.

The conservationists feel that the public lands on which the sheepmen graze their flocks at very modest fees, the amount varying according to the condition of the pasturage, is as much their land as the sheepmen's, and that they should have some say about what's being done there. Over 208 million acres of public land in the lower forty-eight states are available for grazing under jurisdiction of the Bureau of Land Management and the Forest Service, the two federal agencies with supervisory powers. Of this amount, more than 18 million acres—an area greater than the combined total of the states of Vermont, New Hampshire, Massachusetts, and two Rhode Islands—are subject to predator control by federal operatives, who may use poison. Conservationists point out that this work is being done with tax money, including theirs, and they don't like it. They don't want land, which they think belongs to them as much as to the sheepmen, littered with dead and dying animals. When the sun goes down behind the Rocky Mountains and daylight is extinguished, they don't, for example, want the coyote's musical serenade extinguished too.

The sheepman, on the other hand, wishes that every single one of the furry singers would drop dead in its tracks—although he doesn't think this is likely to happen. His reasons are economic. The sheep industry in this country has been ailing of late. Demand for wool is down, in part owing to the development of synthetic fibers. The meat side of the business suffers from foreign competition. This year there were only some 12 million sheep in the country, exclusive of lambs, less than one-quarter of the all-time high. At present the sheepherder's profit margin runs between 2 and 4 percent, and that can be wiped out by hungry coyotes. Conservationists say that small, well-tended flocks do well. But the price of labor is so high that big owners can't afford the skilled help necessary to keep close watch on their large herds. Instead they let the sheep range free with limited supervision, or go largely untended behind fences.

As a result, sheepmen frequently claim an 8 percent, or greater, annual loss to predators, meaning the coyote. Conservationists suspect such figures are inflated. Since coyote populations and their interest in sheep naturally vary from district to district, it is hard to be dogmatic on the percentage of loss. However, several years ago an associate professor and a graduate student in the Division of Renewable Natural Resources at the University of Denver did a year's study on predation in northeastern Nevada on a flock of more than 1,000 sheep, which that year produced more than 1,000 lambs. The project's objective was to determine accurately the actual loss to a herd caused by each major predator as well as to discover losses from other causes. The site was Elko County. During the year the flock ranged from elevations of 6,200 to 8,800 feet. Vegetation was typical northern desert shrub—including sagebrush, bitter brush, and snowberry—and various indigenous grasses—among them bluegrass, blue bunch grass, wheat grass, and Indian paintbrush. The researchers checked the sheep daily through the year, accompanying the herder as the sheep were moved off the bedding areas each morning. These and adjacent lands were thoroughly examined for losses by walking or riding over them on horseback. More distant territory was scanned with binoculars. Occasionally the investigators made use of dogs for tracking. Frequent tallies of the number of sheep in the band aided the identification of losses.

Missing animals—strayed, wounded, crippled, diseased, or otherwise incapacitated sheep—were searched for by backtracking along the recent pathway taken by the flock. In addition, the outer ranks of the herd were daily monitored for sick, slow-moving animals.

When a carcass was found, the investigators attempted to ascertain the cause of death in order to determine which animals were killed by predators and which died from other causes. Among the latter were animals that had died and on which carrion-eating species had fed. Also noted were sheep that would soon be in this category, recumbent animals that were obviously dying.

Kinds of predators were recognized by the type and location of the wounds and the manner in which the flesh was eaten. Tracks and droppings around the body, as well as observations of predators in the area, provided clues. To learn whether healthy or weak animals had been killed, the investigators looked for swollen joints, broken bones, emaciation, and other discernible abnormalities in the victims. Lacking these, a kill was rated as healthy unless it was an obviously undersized lamb.

Predation was low during the early part of the study, which began with the lambing period. During this time and until the sheep arrived at the higher altitudes of their summer range, flock losses stemmed from other causes—stillborn, orphaned, and abandoned lambs; ewes lost to birth complications; accidental death through botched castration, drowning, or trampling in the corrals; death from disease or eating poisonous plants. From summer to midfall, however, losses to predators mounted, averaging one a day. Thereafter, throughout the winter, predation dropped and other causes of death predominated. During one three-day period in February, for example, thirty-eight sheep died from eating halogeton. This is a common poisonous roadside plant in the West, growing three to five inches high and turning reddish in the autumn.

The study showed losses from all causes to total 226, or 9 percent of the flock. Only 4 percent of the losses were attributable to predators. The coyote was by far the major villain, being responsible for 110 kills, or about 3.5 percent of the flock. The other known predators were dogs, bobcats, and a golden eagle. The dogs took two, the bobcats three, and the eagle one animal. Five sheep were victims of undetermined predators. Studies done in other states support the conclusions of this one that winter losses are largely from nonpredator causes and that predation, mostly on lambs, is high in summer and early fall. However, this study showed that deaths of newborn lambs from natural causes far exceeded those attributable to predators, just as, also, there were more losses of all types of sheep, overall, to causes other than predation. Figures from out of the country confirm the sheep's natural infirmity. New Zealand, with no significant predators to prey on its more than 80 million sheep and lambs, reported last year a loss amounting to 8 percent.

The fact is that man's unremittingly selective breeding of sheep to produce for him a creature of maximum economic advantage has created one of nature's more delicate animals. Some of the ills it is heir to have been noted above. But there are others. It breaks its legs in gopher holes, falls headlong into canyons, is crippled by wading in crusted snow. Some ewes succumb after dragging their udders on ice; others, heavy with wool and pregnancy, turn turtle in a ditch and perish through inability to right themselves. The Basques, among the most skillful herders known, say: "When the sheep is walking around, it is looking for a place to die." Western sheepmen, among themselves, wryly joke that "lambs come into the world wanting to die." Knowing this, conservationists suggest that more blame for losses should be placed on sheep frailty than on the coyote. Sheepmen disagree. "I have been raised to hate coyotes all my life," one of them said. In effect, this is the general feeling, not only among sheepmen but among most rural residents of the West. The attitude is promoted by folklore and anticoyote legends. For example, a western Senator told an ecologist that he knew of a single coyote that had killed a herd of twelve deer. The ecologist asked what the other deer were doing when the coyote attacked the first. It developed that the senator had not witnessed the incident; the story was an unsubstantiated tale that had come down from his grandfather. This and many other yarns like it are given general credence.

Nevertheless, sheepmen do have many legitimate complaints against the coyote. Mass slaughters have been committed by one animal in a single night. Lambs have been devoured as they were being born, udders ripped from ewes left to die. Virtually every heinous act charged by sheepmen has, at some time, occurred. Conservationists reply that normally only one or a few animals in an area are responsible. They advocate eliminating these killers only. Kansas is one state that does this. Recently the bureau there reported that in a nine-county area the annual predator loss was less than 1 percent of the flocks. Critics contend that if the area covered was moved only one county to the east, the figure would be quite different.

Still, a bill of particulars favoring the coyote can be drawn. It preserves the western range, where forage is never overly abundant, by eating the jackrabbit, one of its favorite foods. In a year, twenty-five jackrabbits consume as much grass as a sheep, one-fifth as much as a cow. Furthermore, the coyote keeps the deer, antelope, and elk populations healthy. These are game animals and thus considered "good." By culling the weak, sick, infirm, and aged from the herds, the coyote allows only the more fit to survive and reproduce. Also, coyotes are excellent scavengers, neatly ridding the landscape of decaying animal matter, returning materials quickly for nature's reuse in the biological cycle. However, these points are generally overlooked by the sheepmen. They aim to kill every coyote they can.

The methods are varied and none very painless—steel leg traps, aerial hunting, calling and shooting, coursing with dogs, den hunting, shooting with cyanide guns, and poisoning. Traps are staked and buried in the ground along a coyote trail. A bush or weed nearby is scented with coyote urine, a proved attractant. This causes the animal to stop, sniff, and be caught. Aerial hunting is done with a pilot and a gunner riding in a helicopter. It is especially effective in winter when snow covers the ground. The coyote is highly visible then with virtually no chance to escape the heavy shotgun pellets as the craft hovers over it. Calling is done by those who can imitate coyote sounds. The curious animal comes closer and closer until it is within rifle range. Coursing with dogs means using fast, specially bred hounds to overtake the coyote, the hunters following behind in an automobile. Den hunting is dispatching the young. Once a burrow is located the pups are pulled out by long twisted wires that entangle their fur. Their heads are stomped. Or flammables are put into the entrance and the pups roasted. Cyanide guns, called "coyote getters," are pieces of pipe loaded with a cartridge tipped with cyanide. The pipe's business end is blocked with a wad of material scented with a coyote delicacy such as ripe carrion or an animal's brain matter. The pipe is placed along a trail. When the coyote pulls the wad to eat the tidbit, the cartridge explodes, driving a dose of cyanide into the animal's mouth and killing it.

Poisons, ecologically, are the most harmful of all. They are usually inserted in meat baits. Among those used in recent years is thallium sulfate, a compound of the heavy metal thallium. It is a sure, but not a quick, killer. One observer described its effect on the coyote as follows: "The pads of his feet fall off, waste away. His hair slips off. Out in the sun he begins to turn black. He'll seek shade and usually go to an old cellar or back in the trees. He'll be a-shaking all over, and once in a while he'll let out a sharp bark. Then he'll go blind and lose all control of himself and die. But it's dying by inches. It may take a month." The material stays in the animal's intestines. Every time the animal moves the poison cuts into the tissues.

This agent was generally discontinued a few years ago, not for reasons of charity but for efficiency. Coyotes began to avoid it. Substituted was sodium fluoroacetate, commonly known as 1080—an equally sure, but a quick, killer. It is odorless, colorless, and almost tasteless. No antidote is presently known. It was found by Polish scientists some thirty years ago. They were trying to turn out an improved tear gas. When a slightly different fluoroacetate was found to be lethal to a laboratory animal, sodium fluoroacetate was developed. In theory, the substance is particularly effective with the coyote and less so with many other forms of wildlife. But in order to obtain such selectivity, only a small portion of the poison should be inserted in liquid form in a carcass. What usually happened was that poisoners, to make sure of a kill, overdosed. The baits were placed widely and indiscriminately across sheep ranges, including public lands. The consequence during the years of 1080's use was a huge toll of assorted wildlife. Meat-eating animals and birds would sample the first kill and die. Creatures that ate these victims would in turn die. The poison caused the dying victims to retch, and this vomitus was lethal as well. Conservationists, citing the terrible effects of 1080, which was destroying secondary and even tertiary animals, were able to persuade the Nixon administration in 1972 to bar the use of all poisons on public lands. The Ford administration, however, under heavy pressure from the sheepmen's lobby, modified the act to permit the return of cyanide guns to public lands, where they are in use today. The Carter administration, as of this writing, has no plans to change this.

A by-product of coyote killing is the trade in pelts. Prime ones are taken in fall and winter. Furriers describe the skins as long-wearing. Pelts from northern animals are much silkier and fluffier than the coarser ones from southern coyotes. They are procured from many states and from Canada, where the province of Alberta is particularly productive. Demand is brisk. For a three-quarter length coat, retailing at between $2,500 and $3,500, eight or nine skins are required.

Throughout the varied persecution the coyote has endured, it has exhibited the hardihood for which it is noted. It has been said that a wound that would kill an ordinary animal is a mere inconvenience to a coyote. The animal is capable of enduring extreme anguish and continuing to live. Coyotes in fine fettle have been found with three good legs and a stump, the result of gnawing off the fourth in a trap. One went further. She had two stumps for front legs, and moved by hopping like a kangaroo. A postmortem examination revealed she was carrying five unborn young. Other coyotes, scalped for the bounty that presentation of a scalp allows, have revived and gone back to their haunts only to be recaptured later with a patch of bald gristle grown over the skull. A coyote was taken which had its mouth wired shut, a form of maltreatment practiced by some sheepmen. Skin had grown over the wire like the bark of a tree. The coyote could open its mouth only half an inch but had survived in good shape. Another made a living despite the fact that a bullet had clipped off the lower part of the jaw. The jaw as a result drooped somewhat from the horizontal, but full recovery had been made and the animal was in first-rate health. A hunter discovered a blind female coyote who had a litter of healthy pups. It would add to the information about coyotes to know whether she had overcome the disability sufficiently to hunt for herself or was fed by her mate. One winter day a trapped coyote was killed, skinned, and dropped by the trapper into the back of a wagon which he then proceeded to drive to his ranch house. On the way, hearing a slight noise in back, the driver turned and saw the skinless coyote leap from the wagon and start across the plain. "It was a fearful-looking thing," the driver said.

Besides wiring coyote jaws shut, some coyote haters sew up the vulva of the female and the penis covering of the male to get more urine for use as scent. One used to saw the lower jaw off trapped coyotes and turn them loose for his dogs to mutilate. Such cruelty obviously is not necessary to eliminate coyotes. I was curious enough about this to ask a psychiatrist why a sheepman would do such a thing. "Most sheepmen, of course, don't," said the doctor. "Such actions, when they occur, are usually the work of persons who, when young, suffered great physical or emotional cruelty, emotional cruelty being just as bad, or worse, than the physical. The cruelty probably came from sources that couldn't be answered back. Thus, as adults, these persons return the cruelty to things they feel threatened by or hate."

Despite constant war on the coyote by private individuals, states, and the federal government, the effort doesn't appear to be doing what the sheepmen want. Often they complain that there seem to be more sheep-killing coyotes in their area than ever. Several years ago a biologist attached to the Defenders of Wildlife went west to study the habits of the animal and may have found the answer. He decided that widespread, unsystematic persecution of the coyote with trap, gun, and poison could be the very cause of large-scale predation. "I found," he said, "that sheepmen who used the most control invariably complained the loudest about ever-increasing losses. The coyote is normally a territorial animal with a highly developed territorial imperative. Keeping the coyote population harassed and in a state of constant flux disrupts his territorial habits and makes him, in effect, a different animal. This different animal may become a sheep killer. But if left alone in the first place he would probably have never been heard from. If persecution and harassment of the coyote by all present means were immediately stopped and he was allowed to settle back into his normal way of life then government trappers could go in to get any specific coyotes that were doing damage."

However, the sheepman sticks to his belief that he is best

served by wholesale coyote killing. In 1976, the last year for which figures are available, the federal government dispatched over 80,000 coyotes in the West. No total has been compiled for the various states with control programs of their own or for private individuals engaged in the same work, but conservationists estimate the other kills as probably equal to that of the federal government. "Still, we'll never see the end of the coyote," one Fish and Wildlife official said.

The key to the coyote's expansion has been the near extermination of the wolf. When the white man came to North America, the coyote lived west of the Mississippi River on the grassy prairies and in the arid and desert sections of the Southwest. Surrounding this extensive region was the habitat of the two species of wolves that are native to this continent, the red wolf and the larger gray, or timber, wolf. Both successfully preyed on the coyote, and both kept it strictly confined to its area of occupation.

The original range of the red wolf was from central Texas eastward to the coasts of Georgia and Florida and along the Mississippi River valley northward to central Illinois and Indiana. Sizes of wolves and coyotes vary considerably according to location, but the red wolf is generally half again as big as the western coyote. The weight of the average red wolf runs from forty-five to sixty-five pounds, although males of eighty pounds have been recorded. Average length is a bit over four feet, including a fifteen-inch tail. As with the coyote and gray wolf, females are normally about one-fifth smaller. By comparison, a western coyote weighs on the average from twenty-five to thirty-five pounds and is about three and a half feet long, including a foot-long tail.

From the beginning of the white man's settlement in the West, the red wolf like the larger gray wolf was the object of an intensive campaign of extermination because of its depredations on livestock. Too small to kill many cattle, and with no sheep to prey on, the red wolf tended to concentrate on hogs which, in those pioneer days, usually roamed free. So conscientiously did man hunt down the red wolf and intrude into and take over its living space, that, at the moment, it is possibly the most endangered mammal in the lower forty-eight states. Only a tiny remnant of its former range is left to it, principally a few counties in Texas and Louisiana along the Gulf of Mexico. The elusive coyote, far abler in meeting life's present-day challenges, has moved into the red wolf's territory and taken over its ecological niche. In addition, incoming coyotes have interbred with the few remaining red wolves. As a consequence, pure strains of the red wolf are dwindling. Biologists fear that unless the government successfully establishes a red wolf sanctuary somewhere in the South, an effort that has thus far failed, the species will soon become extinct.

The gray wolf, a hulking, powerful animal, is the largest member of the entire canid family barring some of man's specially bred giant dogs. Its primeval range encompassed most of the Northern Hemisphere. Wolves from the northern parts of Asia and North America were, generally speaking, larger than those from Europe, North Africa, and the southern parts of this continent. In North America, when the white colonists came ashore, the gray wolf roamed from the Arctic Ocean southward to southern Mexico, except for those sections occupied by the red wolf and the coyote. In size, the average gray wolf is some six and a half feet long with a bushy foot-and-a-half-long tail. Normally it tips the scale at from 60 to 120 pounds. However, record male specimens have reached 175 pounds. The gray wolf is generally said to be twice the size of the coyote. It has a narrow but deep chest, a massive skull, and broad paws and nose pad. Its fur may range from black to pure white, but some shade of gray is most common. Hair on the muzzle tends to be lighter in color than that on the rest of the body. Ordinarily there is a prominent ruff.

The social structure of the gray wolf differs sharply from that of the coyote. Although reports of explorers several hundred years ago noted large numbers of coyotes that seemed, at least occasionally, to hunt in packs, the coyote under persecution by man soon cut its basic unit to the reproductive female and her mate, thereby becoming, especially when it hunted, an often solitary creature, one that offered a smaller target for man. The

wolf, for better or worse, has never relinquished its pack structure. This is a rigid hierarchy built around the pack leader, a
male; a dominant female, who may be mated to the pack leader
or the second dominant male; the offspring of the pair, which is
believed to stay together for life; and sometimes a number of
nonrelatives. The ranking of the hierarchy is strictly graded and
enforced down to the least dominant member of the pack, the
scapewolf. Because usually only the dominant female breeds,
the wolf is much less fecund than the coyote, But, because
dominant animals are the parents, the progeny tend to be
genetically very fit.

The time of breeding is much like the coyote's. Dens, which
become the pack's home site, are, naturally, larger. Often they
are placed in hillsides overlooking a wide view of level country
below on which the wolves' favorite prey—the large, hoofed animals such as deer, caribou, elk, and moose—may be seen on their
travels. The number of wolf pups in a litter is somewhat less than
that of the coyote, but the young are reared and trained in much
the same manner, with one difference. All members of the pack
play with, and share in the care and training of, the young. This
solidly cements the unity of the pups to the pack. Where wolves
are undisturbed by man, the packs may number as many as thirty
members. But generally they average ten or less.

Wolves hunt by both scent and vision, with the former believed to be the more important sense. Most of the hunting in
the summer, when the pups are small and cannot travel, is done
by subunits of the pack. They leave the home site and return in
a day or several days with food for the young. Much of this food
is young animals and small animals, prey that is available at this
time of year and easily catchable by a single hunter or two. With
this care, the pups mature quickly. At five months, they are about
the size of their elders. As a consequence, in winter they can
travel with the pack. Winter is the time when the band's whole
effort may be required to bring down the larger, older game on
which the wolves at that season feed, including the moose, the
largest antlered animal that has ever lived. A bull moose may
weigh more than three-quarters of a ton. A single wolf can put
away twenty pounds of meat at a meal. But, since it may be a

long time till another such meal comes along, nature permits the wolf to function normally without food for a fortnight. (According to Dr. David Mech of the Fish and Wildlife Service, a student of the wolf and associated wildlife for nearly a score of years, the coyote can go twice as long without food.) Hunting is done over the pack's territory, which may exceed 100 square miles. The territory is separated from the territories of other packs by scent markers, spots of urine left by pack members. Sizable portions of no-wolf's-land lie between the territories, whose boundaries are strictly observed.

Nonpack animals, or lone wolves, also hunt. But their lives are rather desperate. They are believed to be either the scape-wolves that, when food is scarce, practically starve within the pack and thus dejectedly strike out on their own, or spirited youngsters that refuse to accept the places allotted them in the pack hierarchy. Sometimes the loners recant and try to join a pack, approaching it with many protestations of submission and friendship. But that is dangerous business. Often the lone wolf, despite its submissiveness, is driven off, or killed and eaten.

Can a wolf catch a coyote? The wolf's top recorded speed of thirty-five miles an hour is well below that of the coyote. But the wolf has enormous endurance. Some wolves have been seen to catch and consume coyotes; others fail. The deciding factor may be which animal's condition is below par.

Besides being a menace to livestock, the wolf has long had another notable black mark against it in man's eyes. It was, and to some degree still is, considered likely to attack and kill a human being. Tales from time immemorial have supported this notion, and the idea remains today. Although it is true that the gray wolf is an extremely powerful animal and that a single snap of the jaws of a large male could break the bones in a man's arm, it has now been established, after much scientific investigation, that the wolf is not, and never has been, the danger to man that tradition has so obstinately asserted. In North America there is no record of a person's ever having been attacked by a healthy wolf. In other parts of the world the attacks have been traced to rabid wolves. Only one puzzling exception is known to investigators. That occurred some ten years before our own Revolution in a desolate area of south-central France. There, over a period of three years, more than 100 people were attacked and many, mostly children and women, killed by two large animals, both called wolves and each known as the Beast of Gevaudan. They were not rabid. When finally dispatched, one weighed 105 pounds and the other 130 pounds, enormous weights for wolves in France. A biologist who specializes in wolf research, after careful study of all available accounts and records of these attacks, believes them to have been made by wolf-dog crosses possessed of the uncertain temperament and excess energy, sometimes known as hybrid vigor, that may accompany the first-generation mixing of species.

During the more than 300 years that the gray wolf in this country has been high on the white man's most-wanted list, the animal has suffered critically—apart from the routine cascade of bullets, traps, and poisons—from stubbornly remaining a pack animal and thus providing a crowd to draw man's attention. In addition, because of the habitat required by its food supply, it cannot tolerate man's occupation of its territory. As a consequence, over the past three centuries its numbers have dropped spectacularly. In the lower forty-eight states, for example, it is now principally confined to a small slice of northern Minnesota, where perhaps 1,200 representatives of the species still survive. In Alaska, estimates vary from 5,000 to 15,000. In Canada, there are from 17,000 to 28,000 animals. In all, fewer than 50,000 gray wolves remain where, in pre-Columbian days, hundreds of thousands are believed to have lived. Their disappearance has opened up wide swaths of wolfless countryside into which the coyote, with typical enterprise, has stealthily but implacably advanced.

The precise date of the coyote's entrance into New York State is uncertain, a circumstance that is not surprising for an animal that had long since learned the value of being unobtrusive. Probably it was about the first of this century, at a time when the species was enlarging its range eastward and westward, as well as northward. Already it had begun to intrude into our Northwest and into western Canada. Around the start of the century it had reached

Alaska. The wagons of prospectors bound for the gold that had been discovered at Nome in 1899 and at Fairbanks in 1903 were then headed north. Apparently the coyote followed them, feeding on garbage dumped from the vehicles and then on the dead and dying horses that lay beside the trail.

Conversations about the coyote were first noted in New York State in 1912. The first animal actually felled was taken in Tompkins County near Ithaca about 1920. Some biologists think this coyote, rather than being a wild infiltrator, may have been an escapee. People occasionally brought coyotes into the state as pets and for presentation to zoos. Sometimes these animals escaped or were freed. A mass release occurred during World War II, when at least six coyotes that had been brought into Camp Drum in Jefferson County in the northern part of the state as mascots by troops from Texas and Oklahoma were liberated when their patrons were about to be shipped overseas. There were no later reports of any of these coyotes being trapped or killed.

The second coyote taken in the state was shot by a hunter about 1925 in the town of Belmont in Franklin County barely ten miles below the Canadian border. This is believed to have been a wild animal that reached Franklin County, or whose forebears did, by crossing the frozen Saint Lawrence River. Coyotes from the West that arrived in New York State are thought to have traveled through wolf-scarce country both north and south of the Great Lakes, the majority using a pathway to the north because of the wilder terrain there. As a result, these immigrants would have found the Saint Lawrence River barring progress to the south except in winter, a circumstance that could have necessitated long stays in lower Canada.

Large farm dogs that have gone wild and hunt in packs have always been a feature of the more rural parts of the nation. In the 1930s animals were spotted sporadically across northern New York State that might have been either large feral dogs or coyotes. By the next decade, such animals had become decidedly more numerous. Several were shot and sent to taxonomists and wildlife experts for scientific examination. Some of these were described as dogs, others as coyotes, and still others as a hybrid of dog and coyote. The hybrids were sizable animals, usually weighing between thirty-five and fifty pounds. Hybrid pups of a single litter were found to vary greatly in markings, and their coloration ran from white through a gamut of many dark colors to black.

People began to call the new animals by two names—coydogs or wild canids. In the 1950s there were unquestionably large populations of them in the Adirondacks. By the end of the decade, they were to be found in virtually all of the state north of Albany. Furthermore, there was another quite notable development. The animals began slowly more and more to resemble coyotes. Their fur evolved into a generally gray coloration. Their size and silhouette became more coyotelike. By the end of the 1960s these coyote-type animals had spread through the majority of the counties of the northern and central portions of the state. By this time, also, the coydog-type animals had largely disappeared from the scene. What remained was a rather uniform population that seemed essentially to be coyote.

Meanwhile, a bit behind the appearances in New York State, the coyotelike animals were being seen in Vermont, New Hampshire, Maine, and Massachusetts, the states that lie to the east of upper and central New York. In New Hampshire, for instance, the first coyote was shot in the town of Holderness in 1944 by a fox hunter. Within a few years, quite a number of people in these New England states were puzzled by the quantities of these new animals that began to descend on their communities. In 1960, Helenette and Walter Silver, biologists with the New Hampshire Fish and Game Department, decided to try to establish what these newcomers were. In April of that year, starting with a litter of five of the wild canid pups, three females and two males, that were found in a den by snowshoers in the Blue Montain Forest near the village of Croydon in the west-central part of the state, the Silvers over a six-year period bred and crossbred a mixed assemblage of some eighty animals that consisted of the coyotelike creatures, domestic dogs, and hybrids of the two.

Reproduction within the genus *Canis* differs from the common rule. Ordinarily different species within a Mammalian genus cannot successfully mate. Nature, apparently to maintain species purity, bars reproduction between them. There are a few exceptions. The commonest is probably the mule, the offspring of a male jackass and a mare. However, the mule is sterile. This is not true with members of the different species of the genus *Canis*. Cross-breeding of these produces fertile progeny. The key seems to be possession by each species of the same number of compatible chromosomes—seventy-eight.

Chromosomes are the carriers of life's genetic code, which is contained in the genes, the material that determines the characteristics of the next generation. Chromosomes, threadlike structures, lie in the nucleus of the cell, and the genes, made up of thousands of bits of genetic information, run along their length. These bits govern all characteristics of the issue to come—hair color, leg length, paw size, and so on. When *Canis* members cross, the sex cell of the male partner, containing thirty-nine chromosomes, passes into the female, joining with her sex cell, containing the same number of chromosomes. The result is a new cell that has the proper number of chromosomes and will, after gestation, develop into the hybrid young. The hybrid, because of the compatibility of its chromosomes, will be able to mate with, and have fertile offspring by, any other member of the species of genus *Canis*. Sterility, abortion, and birth defects in any species result when some, or many, of the genetic bits do not interlock properly with their counterparts in the newly created cell. Enough compatibility exists between the bits of the sixty-four chromosomes of the horse and the sixty-two of the jackass to form the mule. However, the parts of the sixty-three chromosomes of the male mule and the sixty-three of the female mule do not sufficiently interconnect to yield progeny.

The Silvers, after their long investigation of reproduction and their personal observations, decided that the animals seen so widely in their state and throughout northern New England were definitely coyotes bearing, probably, some admixture of wolf and dog genes. In all likelihood, the former were acquired during the passage through, and sojourn in, Ontario and Quebec. In the eastern part of Ontario, coyotes were seen frequently in the mid-1940s and five years later in central Quebec. The wolves in both provinces are small enough to mate with coyotes. The dog genes could have been acquired haphazardly at any time. This infusion of noncoyote blood would account for the larger size of the coyotes the Silvers worked with. They averaged almost forty-five pounds for a male and thirty-nine pounds for a female. By contrast, six western coyotes from Colorado brought in by the Silvers averaged twenty-nine pounds for a male and twenty-three pounds for a female.

The Silvers' coyote pups were born black. They grew into larger, taller, heavier-boned coyotes than the western variety. The head was larger, the muzzle blunter, the feet bigger, the nose pad broader; there was a cape of longer, darker hair over the shoulders. Markings were uniform though sometimes differing in tone. A dark vertical stripe ran down the foreleg, and usually there was a black spot on the forefoot. The howl was lower in pitch than that of the Colorado coyote, but higher than the wolf's.

The eastern animals, even at an early age, understood the language of their western relatives. Hope Ryden, an ecologist who had studied the coyote in the West, went not long ago to New Hampshire to do the same for its kinsman there. She came across a litter of six three-week-old pups in the house of a man on whose property they had been found. Concerning the matter of communication, she gives the following written account: "Before I left I tested the pups' hearing by playing a coyote tape I had recorded in the West. Upon hearing the wild music, one precocious male threw back his head and joined in. His squeaky imitation of the sonorous wails of the adult coyotes was amusing to hear. I had not expected that cubs could howl at so young an age. As the tape progressed, suddenly all six puppies dived for shelter. One huddled under the sink ledge, another froze midway across the kitchen floor, three made it to a cardboard box, and one hid behind a curtain. During the next eight minutes none made a move.

" 'There's a message on that tape that is coming in loud and clear to these pups, warning them of danger,' the man said. 'Where did you record it?'

" 'In Wyoming. These are Wyoming coyotes howling. They must speak some universal language. At least their alarm signal seems to be understood two thousand miles away.'

"A half-hour later I repeated the experiment. At the same point in the recording, all six small coyotes again took cover."

The Silvers early got onto the track of proving that their

coyotes were a pure coyote strain. They mated one of the first five pups they had obtained to a female littermate. The results were duplicates of the parents. Had the parents been of mixed parentage, their litter, according to genetic principles, would have shown much variation. During their subsequent research, the Silvers found that although dogs can cross with coyotes and the hybrids are fertile, the chance that a hybrid race would evolve is extremely unlikely. Hybrid bitches come into heat in November and December, two months earlier than the coyotes. Hybrid litters are born in January and February. This is the height of the winter, an unpropitious time for young. By contrast, coyote pups arrive in early spring. Furthermore, hybrid sires, completely unlike the helpful coyote father, take no part in the care of these pups. This further lessens the chance for the litter's survival. Although individuals of the hybrid strain may here and there persist for a generation or two, the twin factors of midwinter birth and lack of male assistance with the litter make, in the opinion of the Silvers, the development of a race of hybrids highly improbable. They concluded when their research ended in the late 1960s that the introduction of noncoyote genes had occurred sufficiently long ago for the population to have become stabilized.

The Silvers' belief that their animals were coyotes was supported by taxonomic work done by Drs. Barbara Lawrence and William H. Bossert of Harvard University. Taking the measurements of the fifteen most identifying characteristics of the skull and teeth of the wolf, the western coyote, the dog, and the so-called wild canids of the Silvers, the Harvard researchers, using a computer technique known as linear discriminant function analysis, studied the data on the different animals. The computer matches different variable characteristics with one another and thus determines what species an animal belongs to. After scrutinizing the readouts, the Harvard scholars said the Silvers' animals were unquestionably coyotes. Another study done by faculty members at the University of Colorado at Boulder using the same technique and the same kinds of animals, but judged the subjects on the basis of behavioral rather than morphological differences—how the animals played, fought, exhibited dominance or submission, and so on. This study, too, confirmed that the animals the Silvers thought were coyotes were indeed just that.

At the end of the Silvers' investigation a decade ago, when the subject of their research was popularly being called either coydog or wild canid, the Silvers suggested that its scientific name be *Canis latrans* var. (the abbreviation for variety) and that the common name be eastern coyote. A few years later, another biologist proposed the name "new wolf." All four of the nonscientific appellations were then used rather indiscriminately until 1975. In February of that year at a workshop on coyotes held in New Haven, Connecticut, as part of the Northeast Wildlife Conference, both of the names put forward by the Silvers—*Canis latrans* var. and eastern coyote—were at last unanimously agreed upon and accepted.

Meanwhile, in New York State a study like that of Lawrence and Bossert had been made, using an assortment of nearly 150 of the same kinds of animals. The conclusion, unsurprisingly, was that New York, too, had a population of eastern coyotes. The increase in size over the western species, in what the study judged to be a then genetically stable animal, was accounted for, as had been done by the Silvers, through an admixture in decades past with feral dogs, the small Ontario-Quebec wolf, coydog or wolf-dog hybrids, the large western wolf, or some combination of these. Certain of the western wolves were known to have been imported by residents of New York State as pets or for zoos, and over the years a few had escaped.

With a sizable coyote contingent openly established in the state, hunters feared the animal's effect on deer and farmers its possible damage to their livestock. Accordingly, the diet of the newcomers was carefully examined by university wildlife researchers and state conservationists. More than fifty examples of fecal droppings, the greatest number collected from northern Onondaga County in the late summer and fall of 1973, showed mice, cottontail rabbits, woodchucks, muskrats, and berries to be the things most eaten. Scrutiny of twenty-nine coyote stomachs taken during the cold months of 1971 and 1972 in the northern counties revealed that snowshoe hare and deer were the primary foods. This is the season when hunter-wounded and winter-killed deer are most abundant, and these may have accounted for most of the deer found in the coyote stomachs.

Coyotes are not considered important predators of farm

animals in the East. Being largely left alone, compared with their harassment in the West, coyotes apparently tend to follow their normal hunting routes and prey on small wild animals. Although they have been known to kill sheep, the main offenders against sheep in New York and New England are believed to be feral dogs, which hunt in small packs, rather than the coyote, which characteristically hunts alone. There is no authenticated case of a coyote killing a calf in New York State, conservationists say.

Not as large a catalogue of coyote meals has been compiled in New York State as in the West. But an environmentalist at Cornell University during a fifteen-year period of research found fifty-three different food items in 1,500 samples of coyote droppings collected during all seasons in the Adirondacks. Among the vegetable substances was the wild sarsaparilla. During the summer, fruit and insects account for nearly one-third of the coyote's diet, state investigators found. In the winter in a central county of the state, corn and apples were discovered to be the major foods. In fact, many droppings contained nothing but remnants of these two edibles. Thus, on the basis of knowledge to date, conservationists feel that the coyote in general is no menace to either the deer herds or livestock of the state. Local coyote problems, if they occur, should be handled locally, conservationists say.

New York has far and away the largest coyote population of any state in the Northeast. A census of this elusive animal is, of course, nearly impossible. But a close student of the coyote for about a decade, a faculty member of an upstate college, gives as his low estimate 8,000 and as the high, 20,000. The Fish and Game Department of Vermont estimates the number of coyotes there to be between 800 and 1,000, evenly distributed throughout the state. In Maine the same department provides a figure of from 1,000 to 3,000, and comments that the animal is still very much in the preliminary process of filling in the land's empty spaces. New Hampshire has no official estimate, but its game authorities say that the coyote is common throughout the state. In Massachusetts the estimating has been done by Hampshire College graduate students. They place the total at 500, almost all in the western part of the state. A farmer who lived there until recently in the town of Worthington—a man credited with probably more sight records of the animal than any other person in Massachusetts—reported that often several played and hunted mice among the cows in his barnyard. Cattle and calves paid no attention except when occasionally a calf joined in the frolic, indirectly confirming that coyotes pose no danger to calves. Massachusetts, unlike the other states mentioned, protects the coyote by omitting the species from its game list. Any animal not on the list is automatically off limits to hunters.

I live in the northwest corner of Connecticut, a highly rural area in the county of Litchfield. With me in the town of Colebrook live deer, porcupines, racoons, beavers, otters, minks, foxes. And coyotes. A few years back in the month of December our town constable shot one of two he found feeding on a deer carcass in the woods. It was the eleventh coyote shot in the state since 1956. Another coyote, one that survived, was seen by a friend, Lawrence Madison, whose home is in the adjoining town of Norfolk. Madison, who has spent years in the outdoors as a professional photographer of nature and wildlife, is very familiar with the western coyote. During a recent October afternoon, while he was squirrel hunting on a hill back of his house, which sits in a scenic piece of country fronting Doolittle Pond, a deer ran past him. Soon afterward came an animal he thought was a large dog. It was trailing the deer by scent but it was not tonguing as most dogs do when running deer. "It wasn't until it was out of sight and, I thought, with very small chance of catching the deer, that I realized it was a coyote," said Madison. "Darker and huskier—but no longer or taller than the coyotes I had seen out West."

The coyote has also been reported in southern Connecticut, much nearer to New York City. In Fairfield County, for example, one was taken near Danbury ten years ago. In New Jersey, too, coyotes have been noted in the northern part of the state in Essex, Passaic, and Bergen counties. The last is just across the river from New York City. In New York State, they have been conspicuous for more than a decade in Putnam County, whose southern boundary is less than thirty miles north of the city. Dr. Robert Chambers, of the State University of New York's

College of Environmental Science and Forestry at Syracuse, a researcher who has been keeping tabs on the coyotes in the state for a number of years, has an undated record of one from Westchester County. "Others are unquestionably there, in my opinion," Chambers told me. "But they are hard to see."

Westchester, of course, is considered largely suburb. But it is not the only suburb to have coyotes. Across the country in the suburbs of Los Angeles, coyotes are common. They boldly come out of the hills there to raid residents' garbage cans. Also they are adept at picking up household cats. For some reason, coyotes like to capture members of the cat tribe. They tree and, if possible, carry off bobcats. A naturalist, writing in an earlier part of this century, said: "During long years of trapping and trying to read all the signs, I have found a large number of house cats killed by coyotes. My belief is that most coyotes will kill any cat that does not beat them to a tree. Some coyotes will certainly eat a cat as readily as they eat a rabbit."

New York City now, perhaps without generally realizing it, has coyotes, cat-eating and otherwise, to the east in Fairfield County, to the west in Bergen County, and to the north in Westchester County. Whether, in the foreseeable future, homeowners in that bucolic spot in the northern Bronx known as City Island will be forced to shield their cats from depredation by coyotes is, at the moment, an open question. But regardless of the answer, it seems at present clear that the coyote, neither in the immediate nor in the distant future, will join the company of the bighorn sheep, the Rocky Mountain goat, the cougar, the grizzly bear, the wolverine, the gray wolf, and the rest of those mammals of our continent north of the Mexican border that seem destined to have their range and numbers sharply curtailed by the egocentric activities of man. No, not the coyote—that crafty, intelligent, fecund, hardy, and vigorous animal bred on the ancient North American grasslands.

A Very Familiar Wildling

Wildness is not necessarily dependent on distance from man, as the coexisting coyote proves. An example of even closer coexistence is that of the ubiquitous house sparrow, which despite its size, is a redoubtable and untamed creature ever on its guard. In this country almost universally and quite erroneously known as the English sparrow, it is a highly purposeful individual with, in the animal kingdom, few peers in this respect. Without in the least sacrificing a whit of its wildness, it has, at present and throughout recorded history, linked itself so closely to man as to merit unquestionably the dictionary definition of "commensal": an organism that, while not truly parasitic, lives in, on, or with, another. The role has benefited it enormously. For it has been, and continues to be, a crafty, tenacious, arrogant, and eminently successful form of life, utterly and insolently disdainful as to whether man blesses the relationship it has imposed upon him. Partly through this triumphant exploitation of our species and partly through an innate racial vigor as well as a truly prodigious adaptability that virtually beggars description, the house sparrow —with the possible exception of the barn owl, that nocturnal and generally unobserved predator—probably occupies the most extensive range of any terrestrial wild bird in the world.

Rising above the waters of the globe are some 54 million square miles of land. Of the total, nearly one-tenth lies in the relatively birdless region of Antarctica, that sullen, gale-lashed, icy cap positioned at the bottom of the Antipodes, the seventh continent of earth, too cold and inhospitable for broad-scale human settlement as yet. Its only resident land bird is the pigeonlike sheathbill, a creature of rough habits, which scuffles over rocks and floes along the shore, stealing eggs and food from the penguin colonies. The six other continents—North and South America, Australia, Asia, Africa, and Europe—all have their formidable quotas of house sparrows, as do many islands, some of them far at sea. Of the more or less habitable lands of the planet, consisting of slightly less than 50 million square miles, zoologists have calculated that the house sparrow occupies more than 12 million square miles, or a quarter of the whole. In the northern hemisphere, the bird is found between latitudes six and seventy degrees, and in the southern, which is less generously supplied with land, between latitudes twelve and fifty-five degrees. It occurs at sea level and it travels from there to reside, just as casually, on the slopes of mountains, reaching into the alpine zone at elevations of 15,000 feet. In Europe it dwells north of the Arctic Circle, and in this country in the deserts of our Southwest, where daytime temperatures may exceed 120 degrees Fahrenheit. It inhabits, among other places, Siberia, Afghanistan, Algeria, Morocco, Tunisia, Egypt, Sudan, the Balkan peninsula, Cuba, Jamaica, Canada, Mexico, Chile, Argentina, Paraguay, Brazil; such oceanic islands as Hawaii, Bermuda, Mauritius, and the Grand Comoro; Turkestan, the Caucasus, China, and of course, the British Isles, the source of supply for this country's first birds and the origin of the name, English sparrow, which is what people here still commonly call it. In accordance with custom, many manuals, therefore, list both names, and one, the *Audubon Bird Guide to Eastern Land Birds*, sponsored by the National Audubon Society, goes so far as to omit completely the official vernacular title and give only the popular one, English sparrow.

Literature on the bird often characterizes it as too well known to need description. But it is, of course, a diminutive avian species, measuring a mere six inches from beak point to tail tip, the male cockily sporting a conspicuous, telltale black bib, the female clad demurely in shades of gray and brown. It is, in summary, present in almost every region on earth that is heavily populated by man, with the exception of the Japanese archipelago. But ornithologists acquainted with the guile and past proliferation of the bird feel that Japan, too, may not lack the house sparrow for many more decades.

The scientific term for the house sparrow is the Latin couplet, *Passer domesticus*, which translates directly into "house sparrow." It was bestowed in 1758 by Carolus Linnaeus, considered the father of exact terminology in the field of natural history. He employed a binomial system of Latin names, giving first the genus and then the species, thus providing a method that produced a universal and unmistakable designation that could be used for every living thing. *Passer* is the noun employed by Catullus, Cicero, and Pliny for "sparrow"; *domesticus* is the Latin expression for "belonging to the house," from the bird's habit of being found around man's dwellings and the nearby cultivated fields.

A substantial proportion of the present extensive range of the house sparrow began following its introduction to this country around the middle of the last century to locations across the East River from Manhattan Island, in Brooklyn. The event was destined to be—although quite unrecognized at the time—a momentous occurrence. The tumult that arose nationwide, and continued for decades in the wake of the sparrow's arrival and subsequent spread, far outstripped, both in length and in volume, that which was connected with our landing on the moon or with the Whiskey Rebellion. A sober scientist, writing at the behest of Congress a generation after the sparrow's entry, and employing ample proof, stated that never before had a country been so thoroughly and adversely affected by one bird.

Details as to the precise date of the house sparrow's first importation are cloudy. However, within these mists, one fact stands clear. Engaged in the project, up to their armpits, were members and directors of the Brooklyn Institute. That establishment, since its founding in 1823 as the Brooklyn Apprentices Library Association, its reorganization in 1843 as the Brooklyn Institute, and its incorporation in 1890 under the present title of the Brooklyn Institute of Arts and Sciences, has been generally acknowledged as Brooklyn's foremost cultural body. It created and maintains the Brooklyn Museum, the Brooklyn Children's Museum, and the Brooklyn Botanic Garden. Based on the testimony of one of the institute's directors, which first saw print in the above-mentioned congressionally directed report, the official records of ornithology have, for nearly a century, credited the advent of the house sparrow in our country as having taken place in the year 1850. Now, however, on the strength of a newly rediscovered and unpublished history of the institute, the date appears to have been somewhat earlier than that.

The pertinent facts in this recital, which were in a document dated in Brooklyn April 30, 1918, and unearthed by David Salmon Skinner, D.D.S., follow: "My Father, Dr. Salmon Skinner, was born in Coeymans, N.Y., March 6th, 1818. He became a leading dentist in Brooklyn, having an office before 1845 at 57 Hicks St. and after 1845 at the corner of Montague Place (now Street) and Henry Street. He was an early member of the Brooklyn Institute. His membership ticket of about 1844 was given by me a few years ago to Professor Franklin W. Hooper for preservation at the Institute. . . .

"In 1848 he was visited professionally by an old Sea Captain from England who as he took the Chair found some of the so-called measuring worms (then a pest in the City) on his clothing. He remarked that such a thing could not occur in London as the English sparrows would exterminate them. Dr. Skinner became interested and offered to defray the expenses if the Captain would bring over a lot of the sparrows on his return trip, which he did, bringing one hundred or more.

"They came in a large crate which was carried directly to Dr. Skinner's home at the corner of Montague and Henry Streets where half of them were liberated. Then Dr. Skinner and the Captain took the remainder in the crate over to the then vacant area which is now Madison Square in the Borough of Manhattan, N.Y., and there set them free."

Since measuring worms appear in the spring and, at that time, a vessel's round trip between New York and London could be made in about a month, the chances are better than even that the sparrows also arrived in 1848. The site of Madison Square had been earlier purchased by the city in 1794 for use as a potter's field. In 1848 it had been open to the public as a park for only a year, and the neighborhood at that time was sparsely settled. Thus it may well then have seemed a largely vacant area to the elder Dr. Skinner. In any event, the birds, putative soldiers in the city's battle against its hordes of measuring worms, have left no other record. Presumably they did not survive.

This was the case, also, with the house sparrows hitherto believed to have been the first brought in. They, too, were introduced with an eye to the consumption of measuring worms as well as other troublesome city insects. The Honorable Nicholas Pike, a director of the institute, gave this version of the admission of the species: "It was not until 1850 that the first eight pairs were brought from England to the Brooklyn Institute, of which I was then a director. We built a large cage for them and cared for them during the winter months. Early in the spring of 1851 they were liberated but they did not thrive.

"In 1852 a committee of the members of the Institute was chosen for the re-introduction of these birds, of which I was chairman.

"Over $200 was subscribed for expenses. I went to England in 1852, on my way to the consul-generalship of Portugal. On my arrival in Liverpool I gave the order for a large lot of sparrows and songbirds to be purchased at once. They were shipped on board the steamship *Europa*, if I am not mistaken, in charge of an officer of the ship. Fifty sparrows were let loose at the Narrows, according to instructions, and the rest on arrival were placed in the tower of Greenwood Cemetery chapel. They did not do well, so were removed to the house of Mr. John Hooper, one of the committee, who offered to take care of them during the winter.

"In the spring of 1853 they were let loose in the grounds of Greenwood Cemetery, and a man hired to watch them. They did well and multiplied, and I have original notes taken from time to time of their increase and colonization over our great country."

The Narrows, where the *Europa*'s officer freed the fifty sparrows in the autumn of 1852, is a waterway lying between Brooklyn to the east and Staten Island to the west, connecting Lower New York Bay with Upper New York Bay. It is less than a mile wide. The sparrow is not an especially strong flier. But the birds should have had no difficulty making land on either side. Young sparrows often disperse after leaving the nest. And some are known to cross the south Baltic from Sweden to the Continent, a matter of more than 100 miles of open water. The subsequent fate of the fifty birds has not come down to us. Perhaps those that reached Brooklyn and survived joined the following spring with their fellows in Greenwood Cemetery. This is only several miles from their point of release in the Narrows.

While the house sparrows that Pike and his institute colleagues brought into Brooklyn in 1850 did not persist, Spanish monks that year took some to Havana, and the goodly population in Castro's Cuba today is descended from these immigrants. Pike received his consul generalship in the administration of Millard Fillmore, our thirteenth president, whose term of office saw, among other things, the first condensation of milk, a fluid that in its noncondensed form is fancied by the house sparrow. The bird drinks milk by pecking through the paper caps of home-delivered bottles, and would doubtless swig the thicker, sweeter dehydrated product as well if it could only figure how to get at it.

Pike, despite a possible black mark on his record as the introducer of the house sparrow to North America, enjoyed a distinguished career as a man of science. Interested in natural history from childhood, he early made one of the first collections of marine flora of the North American coast, and it was his background in nature that caused him to persevere in his importation of the house sparrow, convinced as he was of its ability to control insects. From his post in Portugal, he sent back seeds of many plants for experimentation in this country; at the request of the authorities during his stay there, he studied the grape fungus then ravaging the wine district and concocted a method for checking it through application of a sulfur spray. The technique was published as an official document by our government, and the remedy soon attained worldwide use. And Pike was one of those who introduced the process of photography to America. To the end of his life, more than fifty years after the house sparrow took hold here, he continued as its active observer and remained to the last a firm believer in the bird's value to man, especially as a destroyer of insect pests.

Pike was not alone in this favorable opinion. Elias Lewis, Jr., in a paper read before the Natural History Section of the Long Island Historical Society on September 26, 1872, gave a vivid account of the middle-of-the-century catepillar plague in Brooklyn and its eventual remedy. Lewis said that "previous to the introduction of sparrows in Brooklyn the foliage of several species of trees was annually destroyed in June by an obnoxious and offensive worm of a caterpillar, *Ennomos subsignaria*, and that, on account of their hanging by webs from the branches and falling in great numbers upon the pavements, some streets having rows of beautiful shade trees were made almost impassable for pedestrians." Lewis added that later the white moths that developed from the worms "were as numerous as snow flakes in a winter storm." The mischief, Lewis said, was "speedily checked and is now entirely removed by the introduction of the sparrows. They are the chief and probably the only means by which the nuisance was abated." This resulted, Lewis said, from the birds' "use of the eggs, the young larvae, and the moths of the inch worm as food for their young."

The larva of *Ennomos subsignaria*, one of the measuring worms, is perhaps the selfsame species that climbed the sleeve of the old sea captain in the dentist's chair on Henry Street. It develops into one of a large group of slender, medium-sized, big-winged moths whose family name, Geometridae, means "earth measurers," referring to the habit of all the larvae of the family of moving with a looping motion. From this comes the other common names for these caterpillars—inchworms, spanworms, and loopers. More than 1,200 species of the Geometridae live in North America.

The beachhead from which the house sparrow was loosed to launch its assault on noxious insects was Brooklyn's Greenwood Cemetery. Lying only a couple of blocks east of the often breezy surface of Upper New York Bay, the site had been three-quarters of a century earlier a part of the field of combat in the Battle of Long Island during the Revolutionary War. Commemorating the engagement and looking westward across the bay to the Goddess of Liberty is a bronze statue erected on the cemetery's rather lofty hill. Also in this historic and sparrow-hallowed spot is the generally unknown grave of the architect of the Stars and Stripes as it is formed today, a grave that went unmarked until recently. It is the resting place of Samuel C. Reid, a Connecticut naval officer and a near-centenarian when he died. On September 26, 1814, in command of the privateer *General Armstrong* at Fayal Roads in the Azores, he engaged and delayed three British men-of-war carrying troops and supplies to the aid of the British around New Orleans, thereby assisting General Andrew Jackson to gain his victory there. By 1817 seven new states—Indiana, Kentucky, Louisiana, Mississippi, Ohio, Tennessee, and Vermont—had joined the initial thirteen. It was the practice then to add both a star and a stripe to the flag for each newcomer. Peter Wendover, a New York representative, worried about the confusing effect of later admissions on the standard and became chairman of a congressional committee to study the design problem. He asked Reid, then in Washington, to offer his advice. Reid suggested retaining the original thirteen stripes and adding stars only, to be arranged in parallel rows as new states entered the Union. The bill that changed the flag in this manner passed Congress on March 25, 1818, and President James Monroe signed it into law early the next month. Captain Reid then purchased at his own expense the materials for the newly approved ensign, which his wife sewed together. This flag was first displayed on the dome of the Capitol building on April 13, 1818, at two o'clock in the afternoon. A simple granite monument, noting some of the above facts, was raised above Reid's grave the end of October 1956, paid for by a guild of local tombstone makers.

As the cemetery was the scene of the house sparrow's first recognized toehold in North America, I was naturally interested in visiting the place. I arrived on a pleasant morning not long ago. The cemetery is almost 500 acres of driveways, walkways, and tree-studded greensward, an area nearly as large as Prospect Park, which is located less than a mile to the north. This latter tract, however, at the time of the sparrow's coming, was still undeveloped land owned by the Litchfield family. Today sparrows continue to populate the cemetery. When I sought out the commemorative bronze statue and the granite monument over Captain Reid's grave, I found both memorials occupied by chittering house sparrows, perching noisily and unconcernedly at convenient points on the surfaces, busily spreading their feathers to the sun. House sparrows are irreverent perchers.

Apparently buoyed by the belief that the birds were nonpareil bug destroyers, introductions to other parts of the country soon followed, the importations flowing into the nation in an intermittent but steady stream. Portland, Maine, received its first sparrows in 1854, only a year after the successful Brooklyn implantation. In 1858 a number of pairs were brought to Peace Dale, Rhode Island. Two years later twelve birds were liberated in Madison Square in Manhattan. In 1864 others were loosed in Central Park, then not yet entirely finished, and two years after this a major contingent of 200 was let go in Union Square at Broadway and Fourteenth Street in Manhattan. At this point word came from the city of Quebec in Canada that house sparrows were comfortably ensconced in residence there, and between then and a decade later our neighbor to the north reported that the birds had also settled successfully in Halifax, Nova Scotia; in Hamilton, Oshawa, Ottawa, Strathroy, and Toronto, all in Ontario; and in Montreal, Quebec.

In 1867 forty pairs were brought into New Haven, Connecticut, and in that same year a contingent was landed in the city of Galveston, Texas, the birds' first invasion of the Old Confederacy. A year later twenty were released on the Boston Common, and at the same time twenty more were freed in Charlestown, Massachusetts, a mile or two away. The year 1869 was especially notable in the sequence of sparrow arrivals; it saw the largest importation of the species known to have taken place. Officials of the city of Philadelphia, hoping to make wholesale inroads on the objectionable local inchworms, brought in no less than 1,000 birds. That year, too, twenty others came from Europe to Cleveland, Ohio, while in the south of the state sixty-six pairs went from New York City to Cincinnati, whose German residents were particularly happy to meet again a bird so common in their homeland. In the next several years, house sparrows were brought by ship to San Francisco, California, and by unrecorded means to various points in Michigan, Wisconsin, and the territory of Utah. The birds were warmly welcomed. Only a few immigrants who remembered battling the sparrow in Europe were dubious. The majority, on the contrary, provided "nest boxes by the thousands," "food by the barrel," and wished to make the bird a legally protected species. It was an upbeat period for the house sparrow.

Adding to the favorable picture, the wholesale importation of *Passer domesticus* by the town fathers of Philadelphia did, indeed, succeed in eliminating inchworms in that city. In 1874, five years after the birds' arrival, Dr. John L. LeConte, a resident there, published a statement confirming this, one that echoed the sentiments voiced two years earlier by Elias Lewis, Jr., on Long Island. Writing in the *Proceedings of the American Association for the Advancement of Science*, Volume XXIII, page 44, Dr. LeConte stated: "In Philadelphia, and probably in other cities, the Geometride (*Ennomos subsignaria*), which was very injurious to the shade trees growing in the streets, has been exterminated by the European Sparrows, introduced for that purpose. With the disappearance of the Geometride, a Noctuide (*Orygia leucostigma*) commenced to increase and has now in some streets become almost as great a nuisance as the *Ennomos* had been. The larvae of the *Orygia*, whether protected by some disagreeable odor, or more probably by the stiff hairs with which they are covered, are not eaten by the Sparrows, and therefore increase without molestation." Thus, while Dr. LeConte gave *Passer d.* high marks in its role against the inchworm, his observation about the spiny-haired caterpillars of *Orygia* was a matter that was to surface again, years later, to the sparrow's discredit.

While officials of local government brought in many of the first birds, many also were imported by interested citizens. Generally these were of two groups. Recent European immigrants constituted the first, particularly those from Great Britain and Germany, who missed the birds they were accustomed to seeing around them. The second consisted of old-line Establishment figures. Conscious that house sparrows were an exotic novelty, they regarded the bird as a status symbol. Elements of both groups, however, joined forces to become members of the so-called acclimatization societies. These were formed during this period in many places in the country, including cities on both the east and west coasts. Altogether the organizations imported more than thirty species of European birds. These were carefully watched, protected, and fed. But none except the house sparrow survived.

In New York City a number of the elite—apart, that is, from the steadily supportive Brooklyn Institute clique—were conspicuously partial to the house sparrow. Around Madison Square in the 1860s lived a number of cousins and brothers Schieffelin, all members of a family that owned a prosperous drug business, one that to the present day carries on under the same name. In 1864, the year sparrows were introduced to Central Park, one of the Schieffelins, not to be outdone by the uptown implantation, put others into Madison Square to add to those already placed there four years earlier. And, on and off, to the end of his life some years later he continued to release new batches in the square. Another partisan was George Templeton Strong, the patrician lawyer. At the time a political, religious, and artistic leader in New York City civic life, and a trustee of Columbia University, he is best remembered today for a series of diaries he left from 1835 to his death forty years later. These constitute a mine of information about the times in which he lived and the moods and local doings of those times, including such trivial matters as the food at Delmonico's, the town's best restaurant, located at the northeast corner of Fifth Avenue and Twenty-sixth Street across from Madison Square, and such weighty ones as the treatment of Civil War wounded in the field. Strong unashamedly acted as good genius to the house sparrow. He lived in a mansion, now demolished, at the northwest corner of Gramercy Park, and from its rooms thoroughly enjoyed watching the antics in the park of resident specimens of *Passer domesticus*, which had spread to its trees and shrubbery from other parts of the city. An 1870 entry in his diary states: "I feed our dear little Gramercy Park sparrows every afternoon from the library windows."

But perhaps the best illustration of upper-class championing was displayed by a choleric Yankee squire. In the late 1860s or early 1870s he brought the first house sparrows into Taunton, Massachusetts, where he lived in some affluence. He had specially constructed in his garden for the birds a large flying cage, roofed over at the top and draped with netting on the four sides. The interior was fitted out with many perches, nesting boxes, and well-filled food trays. In these plush circumstances the occupants soon began to breed. Owing to the overcrowding that developed, the owner ordered his coachman to install numerous nesting boxes around his property and to turn the sparrows loose. They soon adapted themselves there, too, occupying the boxes and creating a sizable population. But at this point the cats of the vicinity, sensing an opportunity situation, moved in. In due course, they were seen to catch one or two of the young sparrows. This so infuriated the householder that the next morning he ordered his coachman to kill every cat in the neighborhood. In the evening when the gentleman drove his trap into the stable he suffered a surprise. Standing over nine cats, whose bodies were laid out on the floor, was the coachman. But, after recovering from the initial shock, the squire realized, to his satisfaction, that the nine corpses were no longer potential sparrow destroyers.

By the middle of the 1880s, however, the general attitude toward *Passer domesticus* had altered. No longer did the public at large regard the species as, to borrow Strong's phrase, dear little things. The bird still had some supporters, particularly among nature lovers. But the feeling of most of the rest of the citizens, both rural and urban, was that the sparrow had become an evil of monstrous proportions. A national calamity, in fact. Many loudly declared that it should be eliminated as quickly and ruthlessly as any inchworm. One of the things that so upset later students of the phenomenon was that this reaction should have been easily foreseeable. In its earlier home in England the sparrow's inimical habits were well-known. A nurseryman and fruit grower of Centralia, Illinois, traveling in England after the bird's introduction here, wrote: "I found that intelligent agriculturists and horticulturists everywhere I went were astonished that the American people should have introduced so destructive and worthless a bird into their country. One gentleman in the county of Norfolk said that in that county they had been spending money to destroy Sparrows for fifty years, and still had to spend money." Antisparrow organizations existed in England as early as 1744. Almost every parish supported one or more of these, which paid for the destruction of sparrows and their eggs because the species destroyed crops. But, of course, man's mistakes are often not recognized at the time made.

Much of the change in American attitude toward the sparrow resulted from the rapid and enormous enlargement of its range, an expansion never before or since equaled by any bird in history. During the years following the middle of the century when the first arrivals had been pinpointed upon various sites around the country, the area the sparrow inhabited increased very slowly. By the end of 1875, it occupied only 500 square miles, and by 1880 merely 15,640 square miles. By 1885, however, it had spread over an expanse of 500,760 square miles. And by the end of the following year, 1886, it held a range in this country of 885,000 square miles and in Canada of nearly 148,000 square miles. A total of more than 1 million square miles at that date thus constituted its new fiefdom in North America.

In 1886 our nation consisted of thirty-eight states, one possession, one federally administered district, and nine territories, the present state of Oklahoma never having been organized as a territory prior to its admission into the Union in 1907. By 1886 the house sparrow held the whole or parts of thirty-three states, one territory, and the country's seat of government. The heavily occupied areas were the states of Alabama, Arkansas, California, Connecticut, Delaware, Georgia, Illinois, Indiana, Iowa, Kansas, Kentucky, Louisiana, Maine, Maryland, Massachusetts, Michigan, Minnesota, Mississippi, Missouri, Nebraska, New Hampshire, New Jersey, New York, North Carolina, Tennessee, Vermont, Virginia, West Virginia, and Wisconsin; the territory of Utah; and the District of Columbia. The sparrow inhabited smaller sections of the states of Florida and Texas and the territories of Arizona, Idaho, and Wyoming. Not populated by the bird then, so far as is known, were the states of Nevada, Oregon, and Colorado, where six pairs introduced to Denver in 1877 had disappeared; the organized territories of Montana, New Mexico, North Dakota, South Dakota, and Washington; the unorganized territory of Oklahoma; and the possession of Alaska.

Although the house sparrow's prodigious and rapid increase in its terrain was a major reason for popular dislike of it, there was another and very important one—its proliferation. It was staggeringly fecund, quickly filling what territory it took over with members of its kind. A relatively recent example may give an idea of its energy and success as a breeder. In December in Utah a few years back a pair of birds took nesting materials into a bird box and mated. By the first of January the box contained five naked, newly hatched young. At the time of this observation the temperature was near zero degrees Fahrenheit. Furthermore, it reached minus fourteen degrees in the period before the young left the nest. During the first eighteen days following the hatching, one or both adults almost constantly covered the nest and young. During the night both parents stayed in the box. Probably in deference to the wintry circumstances, the young, in contrast to ordinary procedure, were practically full-grown before they exited the box and began to fly. One of them, collected in February, was found to be fat and in perfect physical shape. Such fitness bespeaks the species' great genetic hardihood. Normally, sparrow young are fed on animal matter, chiefly insect material. Very little, if any, of that could have been available in Utah in midwinter. Thus, other food must have been provided. Yet the young prospered. Small wonder that the house sparrow, with such extraordinary procreational drive and the ability to fulfill it, was able, in businesslike fashion, to populate the land as it advanced.

Finally, man himself in the United States contributed substantially, if unwittingly, to the spread of the house sparrow. He did this through a sudden burst of technological progress in farm machinery. Only a few years prior to the house sparrow's coming, agriculture in this country had not changed greatly since the days of Piers Plowman. Oxen pulled a plow, grain was cut with a scythe topped by a cradle, threshing was done on the floor of the barn by a man wielding a flail. In 1831, however, Cyrus McCormick invented a practical reaping machine, an achievement that started a boom in the production of other mechanized agricultural aids. New plows and harrows for use by the faster horse were developed. No longer was it necessary to follow the slow ox. Plowing and pulverizing the soil were thus speeded up. With the coming of the practical reaper, only one other comparably efficient machine was needed for large-scale operations in grain—the thresher. This, coupled with the reaper, would make obsolete the time-consuming practices of cutting the grain by hand and beating out the kernels with a flail. In 1834 a really successful thresher, one far outdistancing earlier, cruder models, was constructed by John and Hiram Pitts, of Winthrop, Maine. It joined a thresher with a fanner, a combination that separated not only the grain from the straw but also the chaff from the grain. Labor-saving contrivances had thus arrived on the scene. They made possible the farming of large tracts of land by a single family. The period of peace that followed the Civil War threw open the great virgin territories of the West. Happily and hastily the farmer with his new machinery moved into them. So, in quick order, did the house sparrow.

The house sparrow's spread and increase in numbers and the consequent public outcry caused Congress in 1886 to direct the Department of Agriculture to look very broadly into the effect of all wildlife on the economy, but more especially the effect of the house sparrow. To comply, the department formed a new bureau, the Division of Economic Ornithology and Mammalogy, which took on itself as the first job a thorough investigation of just what the house sparrow was up to here. Almost 5,000 questionnaires containing sixteen queries were sent out to people in every settled region of the country. Farmers and naturalists, understandably, were prominent among these. But so, too, were postmasters, considered likely to know the sparrow situation in their areas. Requests for information were also published in numerous agricultural and scientific publications, as well as newspapers, throughout the country. The objectives were to get not only an account of the sparrows' activities but, in addition, knowledge as to where they were, or were not, present and, in the former case, some approximation of the population density. Today firms engaged in sending the general public questionnaires by mail consider the result laudable if, using a highly selective list, the return is 60 percent. In that era, one far less communicative than our own, the lengthy sparrow interrogations were answered and sent back at this very rate, prima facie evidence of interest in the subject. Counting statements from all sources, 3,300 persons replied. These included about 110 who responded to a circular on the sparrow sent out in 1883 by a committee of the American Ornithologists' Union. These last data were arranged and forwarded to the Agriculture Department by Dr. F. H. Hoadley, a volunteer amateur ornithologist.

From the voluminous replies, a report during the next two years was prepared. On April 14, 1888, it was submitted by Dr. C. Hart Merriam, ornithologist of the department, under whose direction the investigation had taken place, to the head of the department, the Honorable Norman C. Colman, whose title then was commissioner of agriculture. Less than a year later, on February 8, 1889, Colman became our first secretary of agriculture and his department, formed twenty-six years earlier, was advanced to cabinet rank—promotions that in all likelihood were in no wise hindered by the impact of the hulking sparrow report, which meanwhile had been circulating at high government levels.

The report was published the year of Colman's elevation by the Government Printing Office in Washington, D.C., as Bulletin Number 1 of the Division of Economic Ornithology and Mammalogy, the U.S. Department of Agriculture, with the following wordage on the title page, in this arrangement:

THE

ENGLISH SPARROW

(PASSER DOMESTICUS)

IN NORTH AMERICA

ESPECIALLY IN ITS RELATIONS TO AGRICULTURE

The principal author was Walter B. Barrows, assistant ornithologist of the department. Professor C. V. Riley, entomologist of the department, did a section on the insectivorous habits of the sparrow; Dr. A. K. Fisher, a second assistant ornithologist of the department, prepared the text on the destruction of sparrows by poison; that part devoted to trapping the sparrow was written by Mr. W. T. Hill, of Indiana, a specialist in the area; and Dr. F. H. Hoadley, the earlier-mentioned volunteer, collected and arranged material that had been gathered since 1883 by the American Ornithologists' Union as to the harm or value of the sparrow in North America. The last major contributor was, like Dr. Hoadley, a volunteer ornithologist, Mr. Otto Widmann, who composed the chapter comparing the disposition and habits of the house sparrow and the European tree sparrow, two closely related Old World birds, both of which had been introduced about the same time into the city of Saint Louis, Missouri.

The report ran to 405 printed pages. At the end of the volume was a countrywide map showing the distribution at the time of the house sparrow. In the report's Prefatory Letter, Dr. Merriam alleges, probably truthfully, that the work "is believed to be the most systematic, comprehensive, and important treatise ever published upon the economic relations of any bird"—a sweeping claim that, nevertheless, is probably still valid today.

The use on the title page of the bird's incorrect common name, English sparrow, below which there followed the correct scientific name, was not an ornithological blunder. Barrows, the principal author, in a footnote stated: "The true name of this bird is the 'House Sparrow.' The name 'English Sparrow' is a misnomer, as the species is not confined to England, but is native to nearly the whole of Europe. The fact that most of the birds brought to America came from England explains the origin of the misleading name by which it is now so widely known that any attempt to change it would be futile." Ninety years later this opinion is shared outright by the editor of the guide sponsored by the National Audubon Society and in part by editors of most other guides, who normally list both names in the index.

Barrows, in the Introduction, made the statement that he believed the report's deductions were the result of conscientious weighing of the whole body of acquired facts, put down "with perfect fairness to all sides of the question." However, he anticipated the report would not please everyone. He handled that contradictory aspect as follows: "The history of the Sparrow controversy in America shows plainly, however, that it would be folly to expect all friends of the Sparrow to accept our conclusions as to its character and habits. There are some persons whose minds are so constituted that nothing is evidence to them except what is derived from their own observation, and as this unfortunate mental infirmity is commonly correlated with the total inability to observe anything which interferes with their theories, it makes little difference whether their opportunities have been good or bad, their position is unassailable. With this class of observers we have nothing to do. No amount of evidence will change their opinion, and fortunately for the good of mankind it makes little difference what that opinion may be. But the mass of American agriculturists, mechanics and professional men are reasonable beings, willing to believe the reports of other men whose opportunities for observation have been better than their own, and it is believed that a majority of these men will be glad to examine the large amount of evidence presented, and settle for themselves the question of the Sparrow's character."

The conclusions reached in the report, even with the allegedly impartial approach of the authors, were in the last analysis weighted heavily against the house sparrow. In one area, Barrows recorded that the findings of those submitting data were condemnatory by the ratio of 100:1. Figuratively surrounded by millions of house sparrows and convinced by the data before him that the bird was a major evil, Barrows expressed the hope that the information and recommendations of the report would finally lead to the extermination of the species in North America—a hope that today is as far from realization as it was when he wrote it.

Man in this country turned against the house sparrow—to put the matter briefly—because of its numbers. This was the price it paid for its achievements as a breeder, said by the report sometimes to amount to six broods a year. Although for most pairs this figure may well be an exaggeration, *Passer d.* is indeed extraordinarily prolific. Had its numbers been modest, even so bumptious and energetic a creature as the house sparrow would doubtless have had its annoying habits generally overlooked. But in the hordes in which it was present in the mid-1880s, these were magnified almost beyond human endurance. In many a community, in fact, the birds' activities loosed near bedlam.

The year 1880 was the approximate point at which enmity in this country surpassed admiration for the house sparrow. And, with each succeeding year, the dislike increased, spurred by the bird's population explosion. The report's data indicated that rural inhabitants were heavily concerned with the sparrow's effect on their crops and with its effect on the spectrum of insects, beneficial and harmful. City people were interested in the insect question, too. But instead of showing concern for crops, they concentrated on damage to ornamental flora of all kinds, including trees, the soilage of buildings and other city objects, noise, and the strenuous mating habits of the species. Of the last one writer observed: "The incredible English sparrow is the best illustration of *furor amatorius*. The male suffers from satyriasis, the female from nymphomania. In the several years that we have observed them breeding, in two instances copulation took place fourteen times in succession, with a stopwatch record of five seconds for the act and five seconds for the interval." This sort of conduct, publicly exhibited for much of the year by the droves of birds living in the cities at the end of the 1880s, was an unbearable affront to the world of Victorian manners.

Both groups of respondents, the rural and the urban, were

worried about the sparrow's impact on native birds. On this point, well before the issuance of the congressionally ordered report, the hot-tempered Taunton landowner had made a 180-degree turn. Although early an admiring sparrow patron, he had long before this gotten rid of his. Before the sparrows' arrival at his home, many nesting boxes were on his property for martins, swallows, and wrens. When the sparrows he had imported overcrowded with their offspring the cage he had built for them, he had more boxes put up outside and released the sparrows from the cage. However, before long the pugnacious little fowls occupied not only their own boxes but those of the nonsparrows as well, driving the latter away unceremoniously. At this turn of events the gentleman flew into a rage and ordered forthwith the elimination of the sparrows. The method employed was quite efficient. His coachman dug trenches, filled them with food, and fired into them raking volleys of birdshot, which killed large numbers, in the end finishing off the sparrows on the property. But the martins, swallows, and wrens never returned.

Sparrows are by nature granivorous birds. That is, they prefer when possible to eat the seeds of plants, especially those of grains. The Barrows report considered the stomach contents of 2,500 sparrows, many of them examined by Professor Riley, the Agriculture Department entomologist. But this analysis was largely to determine whether the stomachs contained insect material and, if so, what kind. A truer picture of the sparrow's food was obtained from the examination of the stomachs of nearly 5,000 adult sparrows in a later survey also done by the Department of Agriculture. This was produced only a generation ago, when analytical methods were much further advanced. It showed seeds—chicken feed, oats, wheat, corn, other grains, and weed seeds—to be nearly 95 percent of the year-round diet of the adult sparrow. Insects, most of which were injurious to man, constituted a little over 3 percent. Miscellaneous vegetable matter made up the rest. The heavy grain consumption found in this later review was abundantly foreshadowed by personal observations, highly tinged with outrage, from the Barrows report contributors. To add insult to injury, many of these noted the sparrow's arrogance while feeding. Instead of hiding in the center of fields as blackbirds, ricebirds, and other grain damagers did, it fluttered fearlessly from stalk to stalk along the edges. In this fashion, it lived up etymologically to its name—a fact of which its victims may well have been unaware. "Sparrow" comes into the English language from the Old High German noun *sparo*. Literally this means "the flutterer."

Of the 750 answers received by Barrows on the question of damage to grain crops, 562 were unfavorable to the sparrow; 5 were neutral; 183 were termed favorable to the sparrow, a rather misplaced description, actually. In all categories of questioning in the report, the most weight was given to the unfavorable data, for a very simple reason. The unfavorable replies were far more explicit in details than the neutral or the so-called favorable. The neutral tended to be equivocal, while most of those termed favorable gave little information. In answer to the questionnaire's entries, they reported merely no ill of the house sparrow. Usually they were brief, sometimes monosyllabic, replies. And there was nothing in them, as a rule, to indicate either the capability or interest of the respondent as an observer. This was not generally the case with the unfavorable replies.

Wheat, oats, rye, barley, field corn, sorghum, rice, and buckwheat were the cereals considered in the inquiry on grain. In the matter of wheat, the report stated that it suffered attacks from the time of sowing until its storage in barn or elevator. Even then sparrows seemed somehow able to get to it and gobble it. A typical complaint came from Dr. A. P. Sharp, of Baltimore, Maryland: "Being here the year round they destroy the fall sowing of wheat and other grain, and are at work on the young grain in the spring. I have killed them in the fall up to December and have seldom failed to find their craws full of wheat, showing that they must destroy most of the seed wheat, for I can think of no other way of getting it. I have often seen at least fifty on a shock of wheat, as they go in flocks when the young are three-fourths grown." Dr. Sharp evidently was ignorant of the sparrow's ability to find stored wheat, but this fact did not escape the attention of H. H. Miller and other members of the County Farmers' Club of Sandy Spring, Maryland, who wrote: "In barns . . . not a head escapes." Other reports, however, readily corroborate Dr. Sharp's statement of the bird's scratching up and eating seeds planted in the ground. Another witness of destruction of wheat by sparrows was Dr. George L. Andrew of LaPorte, Indiana: "It has already become a pest in the grain fields in the immediate vicinity of towns. During the last wheat harvest I rode over the country around Hamilton, Ohio, and by carriage to Cincinnati, and all the fields observed had suffered for a rod or two around the edges, in many cases the grain having been 'cleaned out' entirely."

With the other grains, the story was much the same. Discussing field corn, J. N. Bagg, of West Springfield, Massachusetts, writing in the month of September 1886, said: "It strips down green corn in the field, sometimes one-third or more the length of the ear, and is doing so now." And from Dr. Fred Sumner Smith, of West Hartford, Connecticut: "I can speak from observation of their raids on corn, some ears being completely stripped of kernels, the little pests husking and shelling as they went along, so that not a shock in the field escaped them."

Among the responses called favorable were these, coming from areas where as yet the sparrow congestion, in all probability, was not as intense as further east. John Allan Terrell, of Bloomfield, Nelson County, Kentucky, stated: "It does not injure grain more than other birds." And from Howard Kingsbury, of Burlington, Iowa: "All talks with farmers in this section failed to draw out any complaint of injury to grain crops."

While seeds, particularly those of cereals, are the sparrow's first choice as fare, at the time of the Barrows report these were not always available. The widespread distribution of the species and its vast numbers required the house sparrow often to find substitute foods. A certified genius in meeting the unexpected, it made the switches easily with no perceptible strain.

The bulk of this nonseed sustenance, the Barrows report found, consisted of the other crops of farmers and horticultural tidbits of the city—the buds, blossoms, and foliage of urban flora, particularly of ornamental shrubs and shade trees.

Taking advantage of his scientific eye, an ornithologist in Washington, D.C., told of damage to ornamental shrubs: "On the 22nd of February while crossing the grounds of the Department of Agriculture, my attention was attracted by the chattering of a large flock of Sparrows, which had gathered in a clump of shrubs, mainly the Japanese jessamine (*Forsythia viridissima*). There were thirty or more bushes, leafless as yet, but heavy with flower buds, which had already begun to show the yellow.

"The day was sunny and calm, and on walking quietly up among the bushes the Sparrows were found preening themselves and nipping off the flower buds in almost every bush. Some of the birds were giving their entire attention to their feathers while others were equally devoted to the buds. Beneath many of the bushes the ground was thickly strewn with the green and yellow remnants of buds, and under a few of the bushes, near the center of the group, they lay so thickly as to entirely obscure the ground, while the branches above were completely stripped of buds, except near the tips. The birds seemed to prefer to sit quietly near the center of each bush and nip all the buds within reach, and no Sparrows were seen eating buds near the tips of the branches, which were so slender as scarcely to sustain their weight.

"On alarming the birds, they flew into some poplars near, where it was easy to estimate their numbers, and there proved to be between two hundred and fifty and three hundred birds in the flock."

On the matter of harm to shade tree foliage, J. Percy Moore, of Philadelphia, Pennsylvania, had this to say: "A lady living in Doylestown, Pensylvania, mentioned to me that she had seen the Sparrow wantonly pull off the leaves of a silver maple growing in front of her house. (August 11, 1885)

"October 11, 1885, I saw a number of the same species pulling off the leaves of the common locust tree. They seemed to be biting off and eating the fleshy bases of the leaf stems. Large numbers of leaves were thus treated and let fall to the ground."

Continuing to look at the problems of the city and addressing the questions of soilage and noise there, Barrows in his report declared this about the former: "No specific questions as to injuries by filth were sent out by the Department, but many observers have contributed notes on the subject, and even the most superficial observer knows what endless annoyance and vexation, to say nothing of serious damage, is occasioned by the soiling of window casings, cornice-brackets, porches, awnings and ornamental work of every kind about dwelling-houses, business blocks, and public buildings.

"Wherever the sparrow nests this trouble is observable in greater or less degree, but it is by no means limited to nesting-places. Very slight modifications in architecture will often suffice to prevent the Sparrows from nesting about a building, but it is impossible to keep them from perching and roosting everywhere. Even the plainest and barest brick front is likely to suffer, for wherever a window-cap projects a few inches the Sparrows are sure to rest, and defacement is equally sure to follow. In the city of Washington many of the statues are more or less disfigured by the filth of the Sparrow, and in some cases the defilement is so extensive that the statues become positive eyesores, the filth being conspicuous even at a distance. Sometimes a heavy rain obliterates the stains for a short time, but so long as the cause remains untouched the evil is sure to reappear at more or less regular intervals. In the spring of 1886 a personal examination of the statues in the various parks and squares showed that more than half were thus conspicuously defaced, and further observation shows that almost all are affected at one time or another. A similar state of things is often found in cemeteries where Sparrows are abundant."

Another misbehavior by sparrows relating to buildings was blockage of roof gutters, pipes, and drains. T. J. Martin, of Waynesborough, Virginia, wrote: "During the years 1881 and 1882 I was engaged in the tin trade in Lexington, Virginia, and having considerable roofing and guttering to do, I had a chance to note the damage done by the English Sparrow. Formerly it had been the practice to put heads or ornamental crown pieces to the down spouts. These heads formed convenient places for the Sparrows to build their nests, and they choked them up so completely that water could not pass down the spout at all, or only by slow percolation. In consequence these heads either had to be abandoned or completely covered, so that there was no room for the birds to get in. In some cases, the Sparrows would fill the gutter and eave troughs with all manner of trash, seemingly using them for a playground."

A second instance of sparrow incivility toward dwellings came from H. H. Miller, of Sandy Spring, Maryland: "It has become useless to thatch roofs with rye straw here, as the Sparrow wears holes through it, apparently for 'pure devilment.' I know of several roofs that have been destroyed in this way in the last two or three years." And a third from R. W. Kear, of Pottsville, Pennsylvania, portrayed the bird as a practicing arsonist: "There is a bar-iron mill situated in a neighboring town, 4 miles from here, that has been on fire three or four times, in which the English Sparrow might be called the incendiary. These sparrows pick up old pieces of cotton waste, which they build into their nests among the timbers of the roof of the mill, and in every case of the fires above mentioned these nests were the cause, either from spontaneous combustion or from sparks from the hot iron striking and lodging in the nest."

As for noise, the best indication of what city people had to endure was given a few years after the publication of Barrows's work in a report to an ornithological journal. The article depicted the great sparrow roost that once existed in the King's Chapel burying ground in the center of Boston. The author stated: "On a mild, pleasant day, when the sun set at 5:24 P.M., the roost was studied from the nearby City Hall. The roosting trees seen from above looked as if their limbs had been whitewashed and the ground and grass beneath were similarly affected. The first arrivals appear at 3:45 P.M., about a dozen in all. At 4 the birds are coming singly and in small groups alighting in the trees, but frequently changing from place to place, chirping continuously and fighting for positions. . . . At 4:15 P.M. It is now raining birds. I have seen only one alight on a building before entering the roost; they are in too much of a hurry to get there. The trees are a scene of great activity, and the noise rises above the roar of the city's streets." At the time being considered, the normal din of the city streets was augmented by that of the end-of-the-workday traffic. To have the cries of the sparrows rise above these at that busy time suggests a situation at City Hall of near pandemonium. The writer, occupying the same observation post, continued that the other side of the coin, the morning awakening, began while the stars were still shining. "The chirping swells into a continuous volume of sound, not the chorus of spring, but a confused conversational chirping noise as if all were talking at once." This, from shoals of birds, "in numbers too great to count," went on for twenty minutes. What the report seems to establish is that the proper description of both scenes would be nearly insufferable avian uproar.

Getting back to rural complaints, the Barrows report stated that, in addition to grains, the sparrow, according to replies from 472 of 788 respondents, damaged virtually every other crop of farmers. Those mentioned were, in the category of fruits, grapes, cherries, strawberries, raspberries, apples, currants, pears, plums, tomatoes, blackberries, peaches, figs, gooseberries, mulberries, wild cherries, and apricots; in the category of vegetables (green, and mostly young), peas just coming up, pea blossoms, green peas from the pod, beans, young lettuce plants or leaves, young plants or leaves of beets, turnips, radishes, and corn, and young plants or seeds of mustard, spinach, hemp, flax, artichoke, salsify, cauliflower, carrot, parsnip, tobacco, and pepper; and finally, in the category of newly planted seeds alone, lettuce, cabbage, flower, and sunflower seeds.

Considering the number and variety of items given in the catalogue, it is small wonder that the Barrows report condemned the sparrow's catholicity of taste. Writing with ill-disguised disfavor (yet somewhat tinged with awe), Barrows remarked that no other fruit-eating bird was known ever to touch, much less eat, tomatoes; in the presence of a bird with such a peculiar palate the likelihood, he stated, was that no fruit of *any* kind could be considered safe.

In the catalogue set down above, the most accusations in the fruits section (better than 25 percent of those proffered) came from grape growers. One of the more incriminating arrived from F. S. Platt, seedsman and florist, of New Haven, Connecticut: "Last year when I had a large crop of very fine grapes, I found the Sparrows were destroying nearly all of them. I watched these birds and found that they would pick out a fine bunch of fruit and pick a hole in nearly every grape. This hole would be so very small that at first it would not be noticeable, but very soon the place would begin to decay, and then the grape would be ruined. I have twenty varieties of choice grapes that they peck and ruin." And from David C. Voorhees, of Blawenburgh, Somerset County, New Jersey: "It attacks and devours grapes greedily. My crop was damaged ten percent this year. It seems to hunt up all the largest and best clusters, and when fully ripe does great damage by biting through the skin. It destroys grapes by the ton." However, among reports favorable to the sparrow in this matter came one from a grape expert and an old sparrow friend. The Honorable Nicholas Pike wrote: "I know it to be beneficial to the grape-vines."

One of those noting the consumption of fruits other than grapes was F. S. Webster, of Lafayette, Indiana. He was a careful observer, who testified only to what he had actually seen: "The English Sparrow is destroying my apples. I have several trees in my garden, and as soon as the fruit gets mellow they peck holes in it, and it either drops to the ground or decays on the trees. I can hardly get a single apple fit to eat; they have destroyed nearly, if not quite, three-quarters of this variety. A neighbor across the way is troubled in the same manner." Later, in reply to a request for more information, he said: "I am not able to state now whether they show any preference as to flavor, for only one variety of my fruit is as yet ripe enough to tempt them; but they almost invariably select the largest and best apples, either because they are fastidious, or perhaps because they can better stand on them while at work. I do not think they attack the apples to get at the seeds, as if that were the case, it seems to me they would confine their efforts to one or two punctures; whereas they often excavate several very shallow cavities, and these are often of considerable area."

As regards the sparrow's taste in green vegetables, a fairly typical comment from Dr. A. K. Fisher, of Sing Sing, New York, follows: "People living in the village, and who have small vegetable gardens, complain bitterly of their inability to raise peas, on account of the depredations of the Sparrow. The Sparrow attacks the plants as soon as they appear above ground, and again from the time the pods are forming until they are matured."

And from Dr. William Weber, of Evansville, Indiana: "They can do great injury to young vegetables, such as lettuce, peas, cabbage, etc. They clean out beds of young plants if the latter are not protected by twigs or branches." While George M. Neese, of New Market, Shenandoah County, Virginia, wrote: "This summer I saw it eat the leaves of young cabbages after they were set, and also beets and peas. It not only eats the leaves of peas, but picks off the tender shoots."

Seeds were the final category of farm crops that received sparrow damage. H. Harris, of Union Springs, Bullock County, Alabama, gave this testimony as regards newly planted seeds: "It will scratch up seed when first planted; it is as bad as if you were to turn into a newly planted garden fifty chickens. What it does not finish when it is planted is finished after it goes to seed." Harris's last remark was echoed by Elisha Slade, of Somerset, Bristol County, Massachusetts: "The destruction of the seeds of vegetables and flowers is enormous. It is begun before they are ripe, almost as soon as they are formed, and continues through the season. Often it is impossible to save the seed from these birds unless the plants are covered by netting. The seed of carrot, turnip, lettuce, cabbage, etc. is attacked before it is ripe enough to be gathered."

The two remaining major points examined by the report were first, the sparrow's influence on insects, harmful and otherwise, and second, how native birds reacted to *Passer domesticus*. Both city and country people were affected by these matters. And the second turned out to have a discernible bearing on the first.

The insect-eating habits of the house sparrow were by far the most controversial aspect of the entire report. People *did* see the house sparrow attacking bugs, including some very annoying ones. In fact, better than half of the nearly 600 persons answering this query looked on the sparrow favorably in this connection. But the watchers, of course, did not normally see the final disposition of most of the insects. Professor Riley, the report's entomologist, assayed the stomach contents of 522 sparrows, taken over the twelve months of the year. Of these, 376 were adults; 102 were immatures, fledged, but only a couple of months old; and the rest were nestlings or birds out of the nest but still under parental care. Insect food, usually to the amount of only 1 or 2 percent, was found in almost 18 percent of those tested. The figure for those with insect material dropped, however, to 14 percent when only adult birds were considered. The younger birds, more particularly the youngest, were therefore responsible for raising the overall average of the number containing insect material. Furthermore, in the case of the youngest, the quantity found in the stomach was up to ten times the amount present in the adults. Thus young sparrows consumed, or were fed, far more insects than were eaten by the adults.

This general situation was confirmed by the Department of Agriculture's study done in this century. But, with the benefit of more than half a century of scientific progress, the more recent report gave a far clearer picture of the sparrow's insect consumption. Officially known as the department's Technical Bulletin Number 711, the report, compared with the Barrows effort a modest one of only sixty-six pages, was entitled *Economic Status of the English Sparrow in the United States*. It was written by E. R. Kalmbach, senior biologist in the Section of Food Habits, Division of Wildlife Research, Bureau of Biological Survey in the Agriculture Department, and was published in 1940. To justify the words English sparrow in the title, Kalmbach, as had Barrows, explained in a footnote: "Popular and generally accepted usage in the United States, as well as the fact that most, if not all, of the sparrows successfully imported into this country came from England, prompts the use in this bulletin of the name 'English sparrow' instead of 'house sparrow,' the term used extensively in Europe."

Reporting on insect consumption, Kalmbach noted that based on the examination of stomach contents of 2,819 nestlings, nearly 60 percent, or a majority, of their food consisted of injurious insects, obtained for them by their parents. On the other hand, in the stomachs of 4,848 adults, insect material, again mostly from injurious species, was less than 3 percent. The sparrow's benefit to man was increased, Kalmbach pointed out, because in the breeding season, when insects are most plentiful, the young greatly outnumber the adults. However, Kalmbach decided that the insect consumption by the nestlings did not outweigh the damage done by the adults, most of whose food—chicken feed, grains, fruit and vegetable matter—was of basic economic value to man. Thus the species, overall, was harmful. In part, the conclusion was based on the fact that the young are nestlings for a total of only twelve to sixteen days, following an incubation period of about the same length. The breeding season averages about 160 days, providing thereby a maximum potential usually of three or four broods. And, of course, after leaving the nest, the newly hatched young very shortly become adults with adult appetites. However, Kalmbach issued a caution on downgrading the sparrow as an insect destroyer. He ended his report with these words: "But it is well to restate one of the findings of this study, namely, that at times the English sparrow has been an aid in local insect suppression. There is a likelihood that such conditions will again arise." This, of course, mirrored the division of opinion on the matter in the Barrows report.

Just as the question on insect consumption was the most controversial in the Barrows report, that on the remaining major question, the sparrow's effect on native birds, was the least so. This is the matter on which Barrows had said that evidence was 100:1 against the sparrow. People did see sparrows bullying and dispossessing other birds. The 1,048 replies to this query showed it. Barrows's exact words on the subject were: "For our own part, after careful consideration of each bit of testimony presented, we believe the proportion of one hundred to one against the Sparrow is the most favorable estimate which any unprejudiced person is likely to make."

Again, the sparrow's great numbers unquestionably produced this verdict. *Passer d.* was then overwhelmingly in the majority when compared with any other resident species of bird. Thus on each of the constantly arising avian gut issues, such as territoriality or food supplies, its natural belligerence, reinforced enormously by its masses, caused it, as a matter of course, to persecute minorities. In bird or man, the prerequisites (normal natural aggression made abnormal by huge numerical superiority) seem to be the same.

Seventy species of wild birds were mentioned specifically as being molested by the sparrow. Some of the reports of damage were gory, indeed. For example, C. Augustus Rittenhouse, of Montgomery County, Pennsylvania, reported that when sparrows battled bluebirds and martins, "I have seen them throw the young out of the nest and fly to the ground and kill them." The list did not include the sparrow's observed attacks on doves, pigeons, poultry, and in one case, a red squirrel. The birds most mentioned as being affected were those whose nesting habits were most similar to the sparrow's—the bluebird, martin, swallow, and wren, all of which like to raise families near man, preferably in cavities or boxes. But the mockingbird, chipping sparrow, song sparrow, goldfinch, crow, grackle, yellow warbler, vireo, robin, Baltimore oriole, black-billed cuckoo, and yellow-billed cuckoo were also among those persecuted. The last four were particular losses in the battle against injurious insects, as they consumed the ones sparrows would not eat. These insects were mainly those whose larvae were spiny-haired caterpillars, most notably the tussock moth (then scientifically named *Orygia*, now *Hemerocampa, leucostigma*), which in its larval stage eats leaves of various fruit and shade trees; the fall webworm (*Hyphantria cunea*), whose larvae make unsightly nests in late summer, under the cover of which they feed on the leaves of a hundred different kinds of trees, apple and ash being among the favorites; and the tent caterpillar (*Malacosoma americana*), whose larvae build nests, somewhat similar to the webworm's, in the spring, usually located in the forks of various trees, particularly apple, cherry, and their relatives, sometimes completely defoliating a victim. While sparrows shunned all these insects, the Baltimore oriole, for example, has been seen on occasion with its head thrust into a tent caterpillars' web nest, eagerly bolting the spiky occupants.

The Barrows report stated that the English sparrow was a curse of such virulence that it ought to be systematically attacked and destroyed wherever found. Six recommendations for doing this by human means were printed in the document: passage of anti-sparrow legislation by the states and territories; abandonment by these bodies of sparrow bounties; the use, instead, by local communities of firearms, traps, and poisons; destruction by the public of sparrows' nests and roosting places; inauguration of clubs for sparrow-shooting matches; and employment of the sparrow as food.

Laws concerning the sparrow in the thirty-eight states and other units that made up the country in 1888 were either non-existent or contradictory. In the adjoining states of New York and Connecticut, for example, the former had recently outlawed the sparrow, while the latter still protected it. Repeal of all acts safeguarding the sparrow was advocated by the report, and a year-round open season proposed on the bird in all its forms—adults, young, and eggs. Bounties, after careful study of the many then in force, were condemned as too costly and ineffective, the sparrow's reproductive rate easily nullifying them.

On the other hand, the general public was urged voluntarily to shoot the birds. An approved method was that employed by the Taunton landowner—a shallow ditch sprinkled with grain, into which could be fired shotgun pellets along its length. Trapping sparrows by nets and other means was, in theory, a possibility for the ordinary person. But the birds' agility and acute suspicion made it more of a job for the specialist. And poisoning, being dangerous, should be left, the report went on, to someone appointed as the locality's official sparrow killer. All conscientious citizens, however, whether they shot sparrows or no, were exhorted vigilantly to destroy nests and to disturb roosting places in order to drive away the birds. Sparrows that had been trapped, the report observed, either by amateurs or professionals, could provide sport if sparrow-shooting clubs were formed, the birds being released in front of gunners who then would attempt to bring them down on the wing. And for the last recommendation, the report held that the sparrow had been eaten for centuries in Europe. Some people in this country, also, it noted, had been doing likewise for a number of years. There was no reason, it argued, why this group of sparrow consumers should not be increased, since the sparrow, in the words of an Albany, New York, newspaper of the time, had a flavor superior to that of quail.

The Albany newspaper apparently was quite right. On July 20, 1887, the *New York Times* carried the following item: "Sparrows are being properly appreciated. Hundreds of them are now caught by enterprising people for sale to certain restaurants where reed birds are in demand. A German woman on Third Avenue has three traps set every day, and she catches probably seventy-five a week. They are cooked and served to her boarders the same as reed birds and are declared a great delicacy. This German woman bastes them, leaving the little wooden skewer in the bird when served. They are cooked with a bit of bacon. She tempts them with oats, and after the catch they are fed a while with boiled oaten meal. She sprinkles oaten meal in the back yard also, and thereby fattens the free birds. . . . So soon as it becomes known that the Sparrow is a table bird their number will rapidly grow less." However, despite this rosy prediction by the *Times*, the sparrow's proven edibility did not cause its numbers in any noticeable respect to decline.

Dr. A. K. Fisher, assistant ornithologist of the Agriculture Department, contributed a section to the report on the ins and outs of the use of poisons. This was to guide those who might be appointed as community sparrow killers. Fisher, himself, did a series of experiments to determine the most economical and efficient agent for the purpose and to discover the proper dose and the best administration technique for the practice. The experiments tested more than half a dozen poisonous substances with cornmeal and wheat as lures. Following the experiments, Fisher wrote: "In dealing with as suspicious a bird as the English sparrow, a slow poison (such as arsenic) is preferable to one of rapid action (such as strychnine), for the reason that the effects of the latter may become apparent in certain individuals while the birds are still feeding, the peculiar motions of the affected birds frightening the others away before they have taken enough of the poisoned grain to insure fatal results. In such cases it has been observed that the frightened birds never return to the grain."

Locations, he stated, should be carefully baited for a period beforehand with normal grain. Fisher added a list of precautions to be used so children and farm animals such as stock and poultry would not be endangered. He ended by saying that the likelihood that the bodies of poisoned birds would fall where they could be picked up and eaten by man or beast was slight.

An unusual impresario, who made a business of trapping sparrows, was W. T. Hill, of Indianapolis, Indiana. He prepared a section of the report in which, using 6,000 words and illustrations of twelve pieces of equipment, he outlined the arcane art of successful sparrow trapping and described how, once the birds were caught, to house, feed, and transport them. He explained his main problem in these words: "The Sparrow, while it appears brave, in nevertheless extremely cautious and mistrustful, and whenever it displays any apparent assurance it has first learned by cautious approaches that there is no danger." However, through his expertise he overcame the birds' distrust to the extent of catching a hundred or more a day. These he shipped to sporting clubs around the country. The purpose of his contribution to the report was to inform those who would also wish to be successful sparrow trappers how to go about the business.

An interesting note on the house sparrow and a closely related species closed the main body of the Barrows report. It was by Otto Widmann, ornithologist, of Saint Louis, Missouri. He discussed *Passer domesticus* and the tree sparrow, *Passer montanus*, both of which had been introduced into Saint Louis about 1870. The resemblance between the two is marked. But there is this difference. Both sexes of the tree sparrow have the black throat patch. In the house sparrow only the male does so. The tree sparrow also is less sturdily built. On the continents of Europe and Asia, the ranges of the two birds often overlap. Where this occurs, the stronger, more aggressive house sparrow drives its cousin into the country, forcing the tree sparrow to abandon the cities and towns, whose territory the house sparrow prefers. This pattern also materialized within a few years in Saint Louis. Widmann deplored the development because the tree sparrow is an attractive creature, much more tolerant than its relative of other birds. But after criticizing the house sparrow, Widmann had this to say of it: "Besides being much more intelligent and courageous than the birds with which it comes in conflict, the House Sparrow has several really good qualities which are worthy of imitation by our native birds. Its diligence is marvelous. After removing their nest in the evening, one is surprised to see the heap of material which this single pair has carried in within a few hours the following morning; and this is done day after day with wonderful perseverance.

"But the most prominent trait of its character, and the one which explains in a great measure the immense multiplication of the species, is the unsurpassed attachment of the parent Sparrows for their offspring. A Sparrow never deserts its brood. If one of the parents is killed, the other will do all the work alone. If a young one happens to fall down from the lofty nest, it is not lost; the parents feed it, shelter and defend it. If a young Sparrow is taken from the nest and placed in a cage, the mother feeds it for days and weeks, even if she has to enter a room to get to it. Many young martins tumble out of their nests, and are invariably lost. The parents make much noise about it, and try to make the young fly up, but finding that they cannot do it, they let them perish, and even if placed where they could easily get to them, they do not feed them. In times of drought many young martins starve to death, being sometimes entirely deserted by the parents.

"While from the four to six eggs that the martin lays, on an average only two young are successfully reared, the Sparrow succeeds in bringing up all the young hatched, which are four or five.

"The Sparrows have traits of character which may set a good example to some of our birds, and I hope they will follow it."

The descendants of those tree sparrows imported a century ago are the only representatives of the species to be found in the New World. They are present today around Saint Louis and in nearby Illinois.

Two years after the publication of the Barrows report, the final decade of the nineteenth century began. Despite the document's precise recommendations and its well-founded fulminations against the house sparrow, the bird, as might be expected from Widmann's notes on its character, appeared unaffected. It still moved in shoals relentlessly across the country, filling the open spaces, dotting the gardens and cultivated fields, and overcrowding cities and towns. Its advance best resembled the progress of a many-winged juggernaut that man looked powerless to stop.

It seems hard to believe today that in the relatively short span of a human generation the house sparrow had become far and away our most abundant wild bird. Following its successful introduction in 1852, it had, by 1886—aided by the importation of fewer than 2,000 birds from Europe and its own redoubtable fecundity—produced the largest avian population explosion ever known to have occurred anywhere. While no sparrow census was actually taken nationwide at this time, the Barrows report did estimate the number of birds for one state. From this, an approximation of the population then in the country can be obtained.

In 1886 the area of the republic—omitting that of the sparrowless territory of Alaska—constituted something over 3 million square miles. In the thirty-eight states, ten territories, and the District of Columbia, which then constituted the nation, the sparrows were present in all or part of thirty-four states, five territories, and the District of Columbia. The total expanse came to a bit less than 2.25 million square miles. However, according to the Barrows report, only about 40 percent of this, or 885,000 square miles, was, in fact, then occupied by sparrows.

Ohio was the state whose sparrow population was estimated. The report said, in part: "Ohio has an area of about 40,000 square miles, or 25,000,000 acres, and the entire state is thickly sprinkled with cities, towns and villages, separated from each other only by populous and productive farm lands which constitute at least three-fourths of the total area of the state. In the larger cities, Sparrows fairly swarm, and it is doubtful if they are entirely absent from a single village of a thousand inhabitants or upwards; moreover the abundant evidence from Ohio shows that Sparrows are found on almost all the farms in the state, and in grain-growing sections their numbers are almost incredible.

"Mr. Charles Drury, of Avondale, Ohio, said: 'In some localities the swarms of Sparrows are prodigious. One flock observed by me in October 1887, near Ross Lake, had tens of thousands of birds in it.They rose in a cloud and settled down on a stubble-field, covering it all over.'

"It is scarcely possible to do more than guess at the number of Sparrows which the State of Ohio supports at present, but keeping in mind the points already mentioned and the fact that less than one-fiftieth of the entire area of the state consists of unimproved lands, it will be perfectly safe to say that Ohio contains at least 20,000,000 acres of good Sparrow country, and that, on the average, there are at least two Sparrows to the acre, which is 40,000,000 Sparrows for the whole state.

"No doubt this estimate is far too low, but it is desirable to keep within bounds in making estimates of this kind."

The report thus puts forth what it considers to be an under-computation of Ohio house sparrows. This undercomputation works out to be 1,000 sparrows per square mile. Extrapolating this figure to the land the report conceded was sparrow-occupied, the countrywide population, if the Barrows report is to be believed, amounted to at least 885 million house sparrows. The purpose of the Ohio estimate was to argue the futility of paying a bounty to rid the state of sparrows. In summary, the report called such a scheme impractical for three reasons: its unquestioned high cost, the sparrow's fertility, and finally, its known wariness, a trait that would begin to operate, the report said, once the wholesale killing started.

Among methods the report did advocate for getting rid of the sparrow using natural means was the encouragement of predators. However, it admitted that the proposal was somewhat hampered by the fact that the sparrow, without in the least losing any of its caution, eludes many of these enemies by intentionally keeping itself close to man. The sparrow, in fact, throughout the historical record, and presumably well before that, has, with extreme self-satisfaction, sat practically in man's lap, even at a time when that spot bore only a slender loincloth or, more substantially, perhaps an untanned hide.

The report, considering this characteristic, glumly observed: "As regards natural enemies the Sparrow is remarkably favored, for, from its constant association with man, it escapes nearly all the perils which restrict the increase of native birds.

"It is generally supposed that cats must catch many Sparrows, but in point of fact it is rare for an adult Sparrow to fall into the clutches of this enemy, and even the young are not often caught. The centuries of experience which have developed this bird into a parasite upon man have taught it how to avoid the other semi-domesticated animals surrounding him, and it is safe to say that cats have far better success in catching the wariest of our native birds than in catching the Sparrow."

Nevertheless, the report said, some successful predators, at least among birds, did exist. When these were known to eat more sparrows than members of indigenous species, they should be welcomed and protected by law, it argued. Chief among them, in the eyes of the report, was the northern shrike, then scientifically called *Lanius borealis*, and now *L. excubitor*, a burly, grayish, robin-sized, hawklike bird with a heavy hooked beak. Its habit of impaling its prey—small birds and mammals—on a large thorn, the better to strip the meat from the carcass, earned it the name "butcher bird" and a somewhat unsavory reputation. Soon after the introduction of the house sparrow, its increasing numbers on the Boston Common caused such an influx there of shrikes that a man was hired by, according to the report, "the shortsighted authorities" to kill the latter. Over fifty shrikes were shot there in one winter alone. Now, for some reason, the shrike is seldom seen in the area, although sparrows still remain quite plentiful on the Boston Common and, indeed, throughout the Northeast, although admittedly less so now than was the case in the nineteenth century.

Other helpful avian predators of the time, the report stated, were the blue jay (*Cyanocitta cristata*), which ate sparrows' eggs and young; the purple grackle (*Quiscalus quiscula*), which fed on young and occasionally adults; the sparrow hawk (*Falco sparverius*) and the screech owl (then *Megascops asio*, now *Otus asio*), both of which were regarded more as sparrow- than as native-bird consumers. The screech owl, operating at night, took sparrows from their roosts in trees, shrubbery, and wall-clinging vines. Predators the report did not recommend for legal backing were the pigeon, Cooper's, and sharp-shinned hawks (respectively, *Falco columbarius, Accipiter cooperii,* and *Accipiter velox* as it was then called, now *A. striatus*). These, in the report's view, caught more native birds than sparrows.

Of course, some native birds were also present in large numbers in the nation at the high point of sparrow abundance. These were the red-eyed vireo (*Vireo olivaceus*), ovenbird (*Seiurus aurocapillus*), and redstart (*Setophaga ruticilla*), all of which thickly inhabited the woodlands; the robin (*Turdus migratorius*), abundant around houses; and the horned lark (*Eremophila alpestris*), profusely plentiful on the grasslands and plains. But there was a vexing difference between the sparrow and them. They migrated to warmer climes at the onset of cold weather and returned northward again in the spring only for the purpose of rearing their young. Thus they were present throughout most of the country for but part of the year. The sparrow, on the other hand, did not then, and does not now, migrate. It was, and is, to all intents and purposes, a sedentary bird, sticking close to its favorite companion, man, no matter what the latter's feelings on the relationship may be. Thus, if the sparrow's noise, dirt, food gathering, and other activities were considered to be an insufferable burden, they were an insufferable burden all year long, unmitigated by the thermometer's rise or fall, by whether the greenery of summer or snow's silver mantle covered the land.

Cold, which routs so many birds, daunts the house sparrow not at all. Even in the most northerly reaches of its range on this continent it remains sedentary. The Barrows report noted this indifference to icy blasts with ill-disguised disgust: "A healthy, well-fed Sparrow can resist, without serious inconvenience, the lowest temperatures ever experienced in the Unitd States." And more than this can be said. Today, having expanded its range to Churchill, Manitoba, lying on the western shore of Hudson Bay 700 miles north of the Minnesota border, the house sparrow in midwinter handles with equanimity temperatures that for several hours a day may be minus fifty degrees Fahrenheit. These sparrows, present-day studies have established, store more fat on their bodies than their southern counterparts. Fat is a more efficient insulator against the cold than feathers, which both types have in equal quantity. And northern-dwelling sparrows today, and in earlier periods, have cannily assisted survival by sheltering in nooks and crannies in man's buildings and, on some occasions, going inside the buildings themselves. Finally, in the previous century, sparrows in general, but in winter northern sparrows in particular, with characteristic inventiveness made indispensable use as a food source of an indispensable ally of man, the horse, called with some reason by the famous French naturalist, Buffon, "the proudest conquest of man."

In the nineteenth century, the proudest conquest of man had definitely replaced the ox as the main farm work animal. By late in that period millions of horses pulled plows and other agricultural impedimenta. They were at the same time the principal motive power in cities and towns. Additional millions there toiled in front of carriages, vans, lorries, hansom cabs, street railway cars, and all the other rolling stock that moved over the bustling roadways of urban communities and on the highways between them. To do this work, the horses had to be fed three or more times a day. Multiple meals were necessary because a horse's stomach is small for the size of its body, holding, on the average, only eighteen quarts of food. The stomachs of carnivores, for example, are proportionately several times as large. Besides an allotment of hay morning and evening in the stable, an average-sized farm or city draft horse weighing 1,200 pounds needed, depending on how hard it was worked, a daily total of from four to twelve quarts of oats, the preferred grain for horses. Oats are very nourishing, rich in starch and proteins and an excellent tissue builder. House sparrows are fond of oats, too. During the horse era, in the cold weather of the nongrowing season, oats were probably the sparrows' main food. Much of the oats came in the form of grains that passed wholly or partially undigested through the horses' alimentary tracts. These fell to the street in their droppings. The grains were quickly extracted vigorously and unself-consciously by the sparrows. But they were not the only horse-donated oats. Sparrows thronged the horses' stables, where they picked up the grains that had been spilled on the floor or were left in mangers. In addition, horses on the street ate their midday or other meals from nosebags. In trying to get the last of the oats, the diners invariably tossed the nosebags upward, a process that always caused some oats to fall to the street, to the sparrows' benefit. Out of cities, on the farms, winter oats also came from stable floors and mangers. But there, cracked corn and other cereals, as well, were easily to be had in chicken runs. A New York farmer cited in the Barrows report said about this sparrow habit: "I know to my sorrow that it lives all winter entirely on grain, for in buying chicken feed, I allow two parts for the Sparrows and one for the chickens."

Grain is unquestionably a major sparrow attractant. In their wintry icebox at Churchill, sparrows obtain it by dwelling inside huge grain elevators, one example—and by no means the only one—of their living with a roof over their heads. Observers in England have often reported them to spend their entire lives inside large buildings such as factories, railroad stations, sheds, warehouses, or naval storage depots. Queen Victoria fretted about the number of sparrows inside the Crystal Palace, the immense structure of glass and iron that was the principal building of London's First International Exhibition in 1851. I, as well as Queen Victoria, have known Sparrows that were indoor residents. Those I saw inhabited the older of the two buildings in New York City that made up the former John Wanamaker store on lower Broadway—not, of course, erected as a sparrow haunt, but eventually, as it turned out, becoming one. The sparrows lived in the complex's so-called north building constructed in 1862 at Broadway and Ninth Street by A. T. Stewart, the enterprising Irish-born merchant. He wished it to be an uptown extension of his much-admired Marble Palace, a vast drygoods emporium that had opened sixteen years earlier further down Broadway at Chambers Street. The uptown store was the first structure in the city to have a cast-iron front, the then new wrinkle in architecture. It was six stories high, and an open well rose from the ground floor to the roof. This was in the days before electric illumination, and the well was to afford greater light to the interior. In due course it afforded a great place for sparrows to fly. How soon they got in, I can't say. Stewart died in 1876, whereupon his associates, Hilton, Hughes and Company, took over. In 1896 Wanamaker's bought the property. Ten years later it put up the store's second building on the block to the south. As a Greenwich Village resident, I began going to the store in the thirties. This was only a couple of decades before it closed its doors in 1954. But the sparrows, I can say, were in the north building when I was. At this time, a fountain played at the bottom of the well and there was a restaurant in the store. The sparrows, I noted, seemed particularly animated during the Christmas concerts that used to be held in the place. But on my other visits they were active, too, flying unconcernedly from level to level, perching more or less where they pleased.

Those who, like myself, have seen sparrows homesteading in buildings concur that the birds are adept at locating crumbs from lunch bags and other edibles. They are also good at finding water in the shape of drinking fountains, dripping faucets, and spots where rain drops, or snow in patches, blows into a building. To some degree, but far less so, of course, than desert animals, they obtain water as well from their food. Their systems oxidize the fats and carbohydrates they eat. These are turned into sugars, water, and carbon dioxide. The sugars and water are used to form living tissue and energy. The carbon dioxide is exhaled with the breath.

On the eastern seaboard, naturalists agree, the high tide of the house sparrow flood was reached in the decades from 1890 to 1910. The area's horses were then at their most populous. And, in addition to the year-round food supply they provided, the bird's various predators and the divers controls—poison, traps, shooting, and nest destruction—that had by that time been instituted by man were unable to check its rise in numbers owing to the bird's procreative powers. As the bird had been longest established in the cities of the East, the density of the colonies there naturally grew most rapidly. Of necessity, most of the excess overflowed into surrounding suburban and rural neighborhoods. But the cities still remained supersaturated. In 1892 Frank Chapman, then assistant to the curator of the American Museum of Natural History's Department of Mammalogy and Ornithology, counted more than 4,000 house sparrows bathing in a puddle near the Mall in Central Park. Bathing often is a communal activity with the bird. The procedure has a practical value. Bathing requires much concentration. The sparrow ducks, grovels, and flirts up water with its wings. With a number of birds involved, bathers are far less likely than a single one to be surprised by a predator. Chapman's note of more than 4,000 of these crowded into one puddle gives a good idea of the numbers present at the time in New York City.

Besides being the start of the period in which the house sparrow was most plentiful in the East, the year 1890 is ornithologically significant on another count. It saw the successful introduction to this country of the starling (*Sturnus vulgaris*). Several earlier attempts to accomplish this had been failures. Today this noisy black immigrant is more abundant than the house sparrow along many parts of the Atlantic coast. The introducer was Eugene Schieffelin, of the same bird-minded family whose members a quarter of a century before had been so conspicuous around Madison Square. Although Schieffelin then lived on West Thirty-sixth Street, he was as bird-minded as any earlier Madison Square Schieffelin. He was president of the American Acclimatization Society, and he brought in from Europe the starling, the skylark, and various other birds mentioned in the sundry works of Shakespeare, on the ground that New Yorkers should become better acquainted with these literary fowls. He had the arrivals released in Central Park. Figures on the starlings involved vary. It is generally believed that eighty were liberated the first year and forty more in 1891. Of the multiple species imported, only the starlings survived—with what results are well-known. In comparing the range of the starling with that of the house sparrow, one zoologist a few years back wrote: "The English sparrow spread much faster than the starling, and its occupation was substantially completed forty years after its introduction. As of now, the starling range in North America is still far from finished fifty years after its introduction." At present, the starling's range in North America is still well behind that of the house sparrow. On a global scale it is even further behind.

The starling, however, very shortly alarmed the American public. It was a highly visible bird. It made noise. Only ten years after its arrival, it was obviously increasing. Still groggy from the blow dealt by the house sparrow, the nation twitched nervously at the prospect of another fertile feathered foreigner. On May 25, 1900, Congress passed and President Theodore Roosevelt shortly thereafter signed into law the Lacey Act, named for its sponsor, John Fletcher Lacey, a fifty-nine-year-old congressman from Iowa. The measure, among its various provisions, ordered the Department of Agriculture to ban the introduction from abroad of, inter alia, the house sparrow and the starling. The second paragraph of Section 2 of the act stated: "The importation of the mongoose, the so-called 'flying foxes' or fruit bats, the English Sparrow, the starling, or such other animals injurious to the interest of agriculture or horticulture is hereby prohibited, and such species at arrival at any of the ports of the United States shall be destroyed or returned at the expense of the owner. The Secretary of the Treasury with jurisdiction through the Bureau of Customs over what arrives at our ports is hereby authorized to make regulations for carrying into effect the provisions of this section." It was an impressive—if pointleess—piece of federal legislation, a knee-jerk response, as so many congressional actions may be, to widespread public concern. It did nothing to alleviate the critical problem—the number of alien birds already here and breeding. Of the two species, the greater burden in 1900 by far was, of course, *Passer domesticus*.

But an agent to assist sparrow control was on its way. Forty years before the start of the twentieth century, it began as a cloud no bigger than a man's pinky in the sky of European technology. Eventually, through the mysterious workings of serendipity, it proved a most effective tool for sparrow control. It is well that it did. Despite serious attempts at extirpation (through firearms, poison, traps; nest, egg, and nestling destruction; the encouragement of predators; the payment of bounties; and the passage of punitive legislation making members of the species outlaws) man in this country since the publication of the Barrows report had been utterly unable to cope with the bird's continuing population rise. Nevertheless, this device (whose creators in all likelihood never in their wildest dreams gave any thought to its connection with sparrow control) was able in a comparatively short space of time to reduce America's sparrow hordes to endurable size. The result was particularly noticed, and particularly welcomed, in cities of the eastern seaboard.

The new instrument was the automobile, specifically that variety powered by the internal-combustion gasoline engine. The name, a neologism coined at the time, meant self-moving, coming from the Greek combining form *autos*, denoting "self," and the French word *mobile*, for "moving." The first crude wheeled conveyance powered by an internal-combustion engine was driven by a Frenchman in France in 1863 at a time when the house sparrow was taking a deep breath and getting ready to fill our borders. This first example ran on illuminating gas. Next year in Austria an Austrian piloted one that used gasoline. Better models were shortly developed independently by two Germans in Germany in 1885. This was only just a year before the worried Barrows was to mail out his thousands of questionnaires at a time when sparrows, in serried legions, were essentially taking over the United States.

The first operable gasoline-powered automobile in this country was put together by the two Duryea brothers in 1893 and given a successful run in Springfield, Massachusetts, in January of the following year. Two years later the new invention was still such a novelty that a specimen was displayed to audiences as a principal attraction at the Barnum and Bailey Circus, just as if it had been a six-legged calf. By 1900 only 8,000 cars were in use here. All were laboriously handcrafted. This meant that only a wealthy man could own one. But handcrafting soon disappeared. Automobile manufacturers took a tip from the arms makers. The early American inventor, Eli Whitney, had turned out firearms in quantity through the production of interchangeable parts. This idea was adopted by the infant automobile industry. Assembly-line production shortly followed. In 1902 the Olds Company, for example, fashioned 2,500 Oldsmobiles. Nevertheless, motorcars were still regarded with suspicion, as well as with some antagonism. President Theodore Roosevelt rode in an automobile through the streets of Washington, D.C., but a horse-drawn carriage followed in case of a breakdown of the machine. Horses often ran away at the sight of an automobile. This roused the wrath of carriage owners. The state of Vermont reacted by passing a law forbidding anyone to drive a motorcar on a public road without a man walking several hundred feet ahead to give warning.

But before long all this changed. Improvements in the automobile and in the surfaces of the roads over which it traveled came steadily. Today, about half of the world's more than 200 million automobiles are owned in this country. In fact, almost every detail of our modern life is dependent on the efficiency of this mechanical contrivance. Thus, it may seem strange to think that there could ever have been a society in which something of mere flesh and blood, like a horse, was equally dominant and just as indispensable. Yet this was the case in the nineteenth century and at the start of the twentieth. The primitive automobile coughed and sputtered its way into this settled, comfortable world. When its reliability advanced, its acceptance grew. Slowly, but inexorably, as its units mounted into the scores of thousands, it replaced scores of thousands of outmoded horses. Automobiles, not carriages, then moved people. Goods went by auto truck. Farmers plowed with tractors. As the number of horses dwindled, so did the number of house sparrows. The food supply on which they depended, especially in the cities and especially in the winter, was no longer present in the previous abundance. A well-fed sparrow can endure a winter of deep cold. But an underfed individual may not survive a mild one.

Automobiles in the beginning were most prevalent in the East, the richest part of the country, and there most prevalent in the cities, the richest parts of the region. As a consequence, sparrows suffered most in eastern cities. They were reduced, especially in winter, to supplementing the waning oats supply with garbage, which, if necessary, they will eat, and handouts from the relatively few persons who still looked on them with sympathy. The result in the period from 1910 onward was less and less breeding stock each spring. Never again would it be possible to see 4,000 sparrows in a puddle in Central Park—or in any other eastern city. It was a deprivation generally welcomed by the residents.

In 1919 there were 75,740 horses in New York City compared with the 108,036 that had been present only a few years earlier. This difference amounts to a decline of almost one-third. If we extend the ratio to other cities of the Atlantic seaboard—Boston, Philadelphia, Baltimore, Washington, and the smaller ones, as well—the sparrow's nutritional problems are obvious. And this ratio seems to be correct. It was one that in those days was evidently applicable to any urban center. In Denver, for example, there had been, once again, according to official statistics, a reduction of one-third in the horse population during the decade from 1907 to 1917. People were not the only beneficiaries of the sparrow abatement. Birds gained, too. Observers at the time remarked on this new mood displayed by the fewer numbers of city house sparrows. In the nineteenth century, when they were present in the streets and parks in clouds, they were obnoxiously aggressive toward native species. Emboldened by a virtually unlimited bird power, they acted toward individual members of minorities as would any unprincipled gang of hoodlums. By using their numbers, they were able to, and often did, kill birds as large as the robin and flicker. However, with their battalions in tatters following the rise of the automobile, sparrows, ornithologists noted, showed a certain uncharacteristic docility, even a timidity, in the presence of indigenous birds. Scholars now are in agreement that the critical factor in the earlier violence had been the sparrow's excessive numbers.

Outside the cities, in the suburbs and on farms, the sparrow's oats supply was lessening, too. For horses were disappearing in these localities, as well. In 1910, for instance, the Department of Agriculture reported 21,040,000 horses on farms. In 1930 there were only a little more than 13,000,000. Sixteen years later the figure had dropped to 8,025,000. The reason was apparent. For example, even by 1919 enough tractors had been introduced into the state of Colorado to displace 16,000 horses.

Nevertheless, food was more abundant for the sparrow outside of cities. Chicken feed, at all seasons, was widely available. So, of course, was food for cattle and hogs and for the horses that remained. Consequently, the house sparrow, speaking generally, continued in much of the country as the preponderant species, even after the popular acceptance of the automobile. In some places it actually increased after this event. A lady observer in the

Southwest stated: "The English or House Sparrow appears to be the most abundant breeding bird in Oklahoma. On 1,166 miles of 'roadside censuses' taken in May, June and early July, 1920-23, in all sections of the state, we counted 2,055 of these birds; this was twenty-six percent of all birds seen, and twice as many as the most common native bird—the Dickcissel."

In another section of the West this trend was also noticed. A second student of the sparrow in the 1930s wrote: "In the Salt Lake Valley, Utah, and other areas where grain, especially wheat, is plentiful in the country and where the sparrows are not confronted with a shortage of nesting sites, owing to their tree-nesting habits, the species has become even more numerous in the rural sections than in the cities. Today the progressive extension of range and the increase of numbers are still in evidence at points in the West where the species has not yet reached its peak of abundance."

Commenting on the nesting habits of this increasing western segment of the bird's population, the writer continued: "English sparrows are by no means fastidious in their choice of nesting sites. They are equally at home nesting in bird boxes, on beams in barns, in cattle sheds, in eaves spouts on dwellings, on fire escapes, windmills or water tanks, and in almost any sort of cavity about a building. In some sections they construct their bulky nest of straw and feathers in exposed crotches of trees. Such a habit is prevalent in the Salt Lake Valley, Utah, where single Lombardy poplars, cottonwoods, or boxelders may contain as many as six or eight nests. About lumberyards or warehouses close to railroad tracks, these unsightly nests become fire hazards of considerable risk. Not only have industrial firms complained of the birds on this score, but at least one fire-insurance company has taken cognizance of this feature of fire risk and has made appraisals accordingly." This insurance company may, of course, have been conscious of some of the earlier fires that had resulted from sparrows' nests in buildings around Pottsville, Pennsylvania.

The year 1927 was a scientific milestone in the annals of the house sparrow. It was then found to be not a sparrow at all. Bulletin Number 57 of the American Museum of Natural History in New York City, published in the fall of that year, disseminated the news. Professor Peter P. Sushkin, of the Massachusetts Institute of Technology, following an investigation that had lasted for several years, informed the ornithological pantheon of this discovery in a highly technical, thirty-three-page, illustrated article. The morphology of the house sparrow, that is, a study of its form and structure, Sushkin explained, showed it to be a weaver finch, another name for one of the nearly 300 species of weaverbirds, most of which are native to the warmer parts of the Old World. Sushkin based his diagnosis on four points that here will be simplified. The house sparrow's skeleton, heavier than that of the slimmer, trimmer true members of the sparrow family, is, when closely scrutinized, clearly related to that of the weaverbirds. Further, it has the horny palate possessed by this group. Next, the young house sparrow in the first autumn undergoes a total molt, wing quills and tail feathers included, as do the weaverbirds. Finally, the architecture of the nest is like that of the weaverbirds, always being covered, with a side entrance, if built free, or, alternatively, placed in a closed space and thus, again, covered, with an entrance in the face. The discovery created a stir among ornithologists. Some wondered, apprehensively, if the common name house sparrow or English sparrow would, as a consequence, be changed to the clumsy European weaver finch. The matter hung in limbo for a while. The *Checklist of North American Birds,* published by the American Ornithologists' Union, is the organ that officially prescribes the scientific and common names of birds resident in this country. The fourth edition, the one before the present, was issued in 1931. It took no notice of the sparrow revelation. In it the house sparrow was listed as belonging to the Fringillidae, the family to which the true sparrows belong, the family name coming from the Latin for chaffinch, the family itself comprising the grosbeaks, sparrows, buntings, and finches. The common name was given as English sparrow and the scientific one as *Passer domesticus.* However, the fifth edition, brought out in 1955, resolved the matter. It noted the house sparrow as a weaver finch, a member of the family Ploceidae, or weaverbirds, the family name being the conventional form of the Greek word *plokeus* for "weaver," since members of the Ploceidae weave their nests, as also does the house sparrow—if sometimes sloppily. It kept the scientific designation *Passer domesticus* and changed the common name English sparrow to house sparrow. The awkward term European weaver finch was thus mercifully avoided. One benefit of Sushkin's discovery was that it relieved the quandary of a well-known scientist. This was the peripatetic and loquacious William Beebe. At the age of fourteen, the late and longtime curator of ornithology at the New York Zoological Society was an ardent collector of birds' nests. After acquiring one of the house sparrow's, Beebe had this to say in his youthful journal: "All of my other sparrow nests are open like a cup, except that of the house sparrow, which is like a ball with an entrance in one side. Why is this?" After Sushkin's discovery, he knew.

As the 1930s and 1940s passed into history, the house sparrow, despite the explosive onrush of the automobile, did not disappear. Although it had very noticeably decreased in numbers from its high point around the turn of the century, and in certain eastern areas there were far more starlings than sparrows, the house sparrow probably continued as the most abundant wild bird then found living within the nation's boundaries. It even remained plentiful in the country's northern region where year-long life was hardest. Around 1950, for example, an observer reported the house sparrow to be more than twice as prevalent as other birds in Saint Paul, Minnesota. A few years before this Roger Tory Peterson, the well-known ornithologist and artist, wrote of the house sparrow that he had found "roosts of thousands in cities like El Paso, Texas." Nevertheless, there had been in the preceding several decades a distinct house sparrow decline. People noticed and remarked on it. The species' once intolerable multitudes had shrunk to flocks of bearable size. It still, of course, ate grain and other crops. But its legions no longer darkened the sky. As a consequence, criticism of it lightened. Furthermore, about this time it began to receive some praise for consumption of a new insect pest largely avoided by other birds.

In 1916 the Japanese beetle (*Popillia japonica*), a member of the scarab beetle family and a native of Asia, was discovered by two inspectors of the New Jersey State Department of Agriculture in the county of Burlington in the central part of the state. Apparently the insect had arrived sometime earlier in the earth surrounding the roots of ornamental plants imported from Japan, most likely Japanese iris or azalea. The beetle, an extremely serious enemy of flora, is a chunky bug less than half an inch long and about a quarter of an inch wide with metallic green oval body and coppery wing covers. The New Jersey inspectors at the time of their discovery found only a dozen individuals. But by three years later an entomologist wrote that the invaders had increased near the point of their original detection to such an extent that 20,000 of them could "be collected by hand by one person in a single day." By 1934 the beetles had broken through quarantine lines and at present have spread over much of the country. The annual damage they cause has been estimated at more than $10 million. The adults, whose life is six weeks, skeletonize the leaves of over 200 kinds of plants and consume fruits such as peaches. The larvae, which dwell underground for ten months of the year, feed on the roots of plants, including grasses, and thus can be particularly hard on golf greens.

Most birds that eat insects wouldn't take a second look at the Japanese beetle. Not so the house sparrow. One naturalist wrote: "The English sparrow is one of the heaviest bird feeders on the Japanese beetles, which have become such a pest in parts of the East. It is the most versatile bird in its hunting of them, too. It flies to commanding perches on rose bushes and trellises, scans the leaves and flowers thoroughly, and upon locating a beetle makes its capture with a swoop. It searches the bushes from below, hopping along the flower beds, peering intently and then darting upward to seize its prey. I have seen it make catches as high as eighteen feet up in trees. It also pursues low-flying beetles through the air and captures them on the wing."

Other harmful insects devoured by the house sparrow include plant lice or aphids, tiny bugs of the family Aphididae, which suck the juices of plants, and cutworms, larvae of some of the 2,200 North American species of noctuid moths (family name Noctuidae), which feed on roots and shoots of plants and have the noxious habit of often cutting off the stem just above the ground. Another blight the house sparrow preys on is the armyworm (*Cirphis unipuncta*); its numbers may be so large that all available food, chiefly grasses, in the area the worm occupies is

eaten, and the infestation, like an army, must move on. The introduced alfalfa beetle (*Hypera posticus*) is also a quarry. A European snout beetle, it is highly destructive to alfalfa, whose leaves
it consumes. The cabbageworm (*Pieris rapae*), the larva of the
very common small, white cabbage butterfly, is garnered, too. It
is a serious pest of the cabbage plant, but not if the house sparrow
can reach it first. Many of the short-horned grasshoppers of the
very injurious genus *Melanopolus* are also taken. These grasshoppers are technically locusts—great feeders on all kinds of
greenery. They are the insects responsible for the plagues of
locusts mentioned in the Bible.

The house sparrow has not, to date, balanced accounts with
the automobile. But it took a step in that direction around the
middle of this century. At that time the radiators of cars were
designed with a front that had a metal honeycomb. Because of
the relatively high speeds at which the machines could be driven,
the grilles in warm weather caught and held numerous insects.
Not only here but also in Western Europe, observers began reporting house sparrows assiduously stripping the radiators of
parked automobiles of a tasty assortment of toasted moths, wasps,
June bugs, and damselflies. While today's automobiles no longer
provide the sparrow with these tidbits, the marked increase in
this country of horses for riding may soon more than offset the
loss.

In June 1960, at the urging of the Department of the Interior,
the House Judiciary Committee approved legislation lifting the
embargo on importation of the house sparrow to this country.
This was the ban that had been imposed sixty years earlier by one
of the provisions of the Lacey Act. Evidently someone in authority
at Interior looked out the window and realized, with a sudden
flash of insight, that the arrival of a few more house sparrows
from overseas would make precious little difference to the
thousands already present in the District of Columbia. Soon
thereafter Congress passed the Judiciary Committee bill, and the
house sparrow was free once more legally to enter the country.

Several years later the house sparrow was again in the news.
Through the research of two scientists at the University of Kansas,
the bird made an important contribution to biological literature.

Prior to this study it had been thought that any physical change in an avian species would require at a minimum a span upward of 4,000 years. However, these investigators stated that within the space of less than a century—perhaps in as little as fifty years —house sparrows in the western part of North America had formed two distinct races. Technically, a race is a group within a species having similar characteristics that do not distinguish it from the specific type sufficiently to form a separate species. The house sparrow races met this meaning. Both also complied with Gloger's rule. This is a biological precept that states that animals in moist northern areas tend to be heavier and darker in color than their fellows in dry southern regions. The two races of *Passer d.* conformed. Individuals in the wet northwest corner of the country and its neighboring Canadian terrain were darkly pigmented, those from Vancouver, British Columbia, where the bird arrived in 1900, being especially dark. Also they were heavier than their slighter, lighter-colored counterparts in the dry Southwest of the United States, those from Death Valley, California, to which the bird came in 1914, having attained an extreme in pallor. So sudden a variation, never before recorded in science, was doubtless the result of geographical circumstances that were unique. Across a continent originally utterly devoid of house sparrows, profuse numbers of them spread quickly, the wide environmental differences of the terrain causing quick changes in the breeding stock. In a land already supplied with a native population of the species, such a rapid differentiation would have been impossible, zoologists believe.

Weaverbirds, the stock from which the house sparrow sprang, are natives of Africa and Eurasia. The 275 species are all diurnal and terrestrial. Most are short-legged. The plumage has a wide variety of colors, many patterns being bold and conspicuously barred or spotted. The habitat is woods, scrub, or arid bush; the preferred food, seeds or insects. The birds are gregarious, both parents care for the young, and some species are strikingly colonial. The nests are the family's most spectacular feature, through the formation of which, by the use of weaving, the group gets its name. To those who think of birds' nests as simple structures, many of the constructions of the Ploceidae—the most artfully woven, complicated, and, relative to the size of the builders, by far the largest in the world—would come as astonishing surprises. Protective placement is common. Some species regularly build over water, near the eyries of predators, or close to the nests of wasps. Advanced weavers make nests using knots. A two-foot-long tunnel entrance to thwart tree-climbing snakes is the feature of another. Perhaps the example leading all others in singularity is the vast nest, one of the most intricate pieces of avian workmanship known, produced by the social weaver of South Africa (*Philetarius socius*), a bird with the same general proportions of, but just a mite smaller than, the house sparrow. As many as 300 pairs may team up to build a massive platform of grass on the boughs of an isolated tree on the veldt. Beneath this ceiling, somehow using their short bills efficiently for the task, they weave a thick underpinning of grass and straw pitted with upright tunnels. Each tunnel ends at the top in a bulbous nest chamber, one chamber for a pair. One of these multichambered nests measured twenty by thirty feet, by five feet deep. The total fabrications have been known to weigh hundreds of pounds.

Although in this country the house sparrow unquestionably caused enormous damage during the nineteenth century, the most destructive bird in the world today is its cousin, the red-billed quelea (*Quelea quelea*). This is a five-inch-long weaverbird with red bill, black mask, and pink hood and breast. Its wings, back, and tail, however, are much like those of the house sparrow. The quelea, a highly gregarious species, in some years irrupts in astronomical numbers from its breeding grounds in tropical Africa. It then undertakes huge migrations to the south, drawn by the mass cultivation of grain that has recently taken the place of the many small subsistence farms of the old days. The ability of the young queleas to reproduce before they are one year old, a trait shared by the house sparrow, assists the population explosions. Throughout its huge flocks the moment of breeding is simultaneous, keyed to the onset of seasonal rains. At times the nests of a flock are in every tree over several thousand acres, 10 million of them having been estimated in such an area. Students who have studied the bird in Senegal report that as many as 5,000 nests may be in a single tree. Since throughout the colonies the laying of eggs and the incubation process take place at the same time, when the broken shells of the hatchlings are pushed from the nest by the parent birds, they resemble the fall of snowflakes in a wintry storm. After fledging, a large colony may contain 40 million individuals, making the quelea the most numerous of social birds since the days of the passenger pigeon. The irruptions of the queleas to the south have been compared to the disastrous plagues of short-horned grasshoppers or the mass migrations of the lemmings in northern Europe. Inhabitants of the invaded regions fight the queleas, usually with organophosphorus poison sprays, a family of agents that act by inhibiting cholinesterase, essential to, among other things, the functioning of the liver, thus causing death. But flamethrowers, poison gas, and explosives are also used against the birds, in both the countries to which they migrate and those in which they have their nests.

Just as man's population center in the United States has moved steadily westward over the years, so has that of his uninvited associate, the house sparrow. It is now miles further in that direction than it was three-quarters of a century ago. The sparrow's center of abundance today stretches from Ohio and southern Michigan westward to Nebraska. Other areas of density are Maryland, western Mississippi, eastern Kansas, northern and southern Texas, and central California. The sparsest settled territory is the Rocky Mountain section ranging southward from Montana through northern Arizona. Cities and towns of any size in this region all have plenty of sparrows. But outside of them, where there are few human beings, there are few sparrows. So far as has been reported to date, the bird has not penetrated to our largest state, Alaska. This is a bit odd. For the bird occurs at Two Rivers Indian Village in the Mackenzie District of the Northwest Territory of central Canada, which is more than 700 miles further north than the southernmost part of Alaska. However, *Passer domesticus* is known to be moving slowly north from central British Columbia along the coast, a path that seems bound soon to take the species into the southern tip of Alaska.

Worldwide the range of the house sparrow is unquestionably still increasing. The best official report of the area it occupied some twenty years ago is in the American Ornithologists' Union's *Checklist of North American Birds*, issued in 1955 and based on observations by ornithological correspondents here and abroad. This disclosed that the house sparrow in the northern hemisphere of the New World inhabited the lower forty-eight states of the United States, reached well into northern Canada, colonized Bermuda and several of the major Caribbean islands, and had gotten as far south in Mexico as the states of Guerrero and Vera Cruz south of Mexico City. In South America the main settlements were in the southern part of the continent—Chile, Argentina, Paraguay, Uruguay, and southeastern Brazil. The bird had also reached the Falkland Islands, 500 miles off the mainland, by hitching a ride on a sheep boat that had earlier discharged cargo on the eastern coast.

In the northern hemisphere of the Old World, according to the *Checklist*, the house sparrow was solidly entrenched across much of the entire expanse of Eurasia. Most of southern Europe was also its domain, as was northern Africa. In Asia it descended to Iran, Arabia, India, Burma, and Ceylon in the south. Below the equator in the Old World it was established in Mombasa in Kenya, at the tip of South Africa, and in such islands as Zanzibar, Mauritius, the Grand Comoro, Australia, and New Zealand.

Since the publication of the *Checklist*, the following extensions of the habitat of the house sparrow are known to have occurred. Northward progress has continued slow but steady in North America. To the south, according to Dr. Eugene Eisenmann, of the American Museum of Natural History in New York City, who keeps an eye on birds in Latin America, the house sparrow has been seen recently in Guatemala, El Salvador, Costa Rica, and western Panama—almost to the doorstep of South America, a jump of about 2,000 miles since the *Checklist* came out. In South America itself the bird has enlarged its living space in Brazil and gone further northward into Bolivia and Peru.

In that portion of Africa lying in the southern hemisphere the house sparrow also has notably increased its terrain. When the *Checklist* appeared, the bird had spread between East London and Durban, the two ports on the South African coast where it had been introduced about 1890, and had moved westward into parts of the provinces of Cape, Natal, and the Orange Free State.

In the little more than two decades since then, it has occupied most of the Republic of South Africa, has gone west as far as southern Namibia (formerly South-west Africa), and northward in southeast Africa through parts of Lesotho (formerly Basuto-land), Rhodesia, Mozambique, Zambia, and Malawi, a jump of more than 2,000 miles through the interior of southeastern Africa. Normally, when widening its environment, the sparrow for its own convenience elects to stick closely to man. But in range widening it is not all that slavishly dependent on him. An article a few years back in an Australian ornithological journal makes this clear. It revealed that certain rugged individualists, pioneer types, in the form of isolated pairs, dwell and do very nicely, thank you, in the treeless, saltbush country of the hot outback of Australia, where they may not see a man from one year's end to the next, the anomaly constituting an atypical footnote to house sparrow range extension.

A farflung outpost of the sparrow in the southern hemisphere of the Old World is Campbell Island, a lonely speck of land 400 miles south of New Zealand in the direction of Antarctica. Presumably the first sparrows arrived by hitching a ride on a ship, a common practice of theirs. A house sparrow's nest there is the most southerly that has ben spotted by Roger Tory Peterson during a lifetime of ornithological research.

The *New York Times* in 1927 ran an article on the global reach of the house sparrow. The item stated that flocks were advancing into new territory at the rate of twenty miles a year and that half of the inhabited areas of the earth were said to be occupied by them. While the first point may or may not be correct, the second seems, if only at the moment, to be an overstatement. However, taking a look back at developments over the past few years, it seems quite possible that the house sparrow—so full of adaptability, guile, and vitality—may, given a few additional years—or a few additional decades—indeed occupy half—or more than half—of the areas on earth where man abides.

Very few of the world's more than 8,000 species of wild birds are known by name to the average American. But the house, or

English, sparrow most certainly is. And across its broadly cosmopolitan range around the rest of the globe it is, to most of the persons living there, equally well known. Were there no other proof than this, such widespread recognition of the bird would bespeak a protracted contact with human beings. For, among the general public, there is, quite frankly, an intense grassroots indifference to bird identification.

The pigeon and the starling are also usually called by name. But the contacts of these two with our species have been conspicuously brief compared with that of the house sparrow, whose involvement with man dates back to well before history itself had dawned.

The relationship, however, is a classic example of a purely one-sided association. It was initiated, and has since been rigidly imposed, by the house sparrow, an egregiously strong-willed character. But the proximity has also produced in man certain reactions that doubtless would never have occurred in a looser linkage. Some of these would, indeed, to the average reader seem to be quite singular or outré. However, it must be remembered that of all the thousands of wild bird species, none, because of the sparrow's prolonged propinquity to human beings, has been the object of so much research. This, when undertaken in quantity, can breed forms that could well surprise the man in the street. A pertinent example of such offbeat work was the enumeration a few years back of the number of feathers to be found on the exterior part of an adult male house sparrow's plumage.

The study was based on an examination of eight birds. Only such feathers as formed portions of the exterior coat were counted. Left out were what essentially constitute the undercoat —the downy plumules and hairlike filoplumes whose function is to provide insulation. In winter the house sparrow was found to have 3,615 feathers. This was at a time when the annual molt had been completed several months earlier. In summer, as might have been expected, the count was less, some feathers having been lost through normal wear and tear, in fights, and doubtless through having been dropped because of higher temperatures. The total then was 3,158 feathers.

Feathers do not grow haphazardly on a bird, but follow

definite patterns. The skin is divided between regions where feathers grow, pterylae, and regions where they do not, apteria. The study of feather patterns is called pterylology. A house sparrow's feathers are of various kinds. The more important sprout from the back, the underbody, the wings, and the tail. Those on the back grow in three elements, shaped like the chevrons on a sergeant's sleeve. The points of the inverted Vs lie over the backbone, and the elements cover the back from the neck to the rump. The total of the three sections, which are separated by spaces, makes up thirty-three rows of feathers. On the underbody, coverage is accomplished by four elements, two on each side, running from the upper breast to the anus. The larger of each pair is a crescent, starting at the upper breast and continuing down in a series of inverted V-shaped rows along the side of the body. A separation exists near the middle before the rows start again. The smaller element is made up of straight lines, which begin inside the crescent. It reaches its maximum width of four feathers below the separation and ends at row thirty-nine of the crescent just before, and to one side of, the anus. The wing feathers in descending order of size are the primaries, the secondaries, the tertiaries, and those of the alula, or bastard wing. The house sparrow has ten primaries, a point that assisted its placement as a weaverbird, not a sparrow. The true sparrows, natives of the Old World, have nine primaries. The New World birds that we call sparrows—the song sparrow, the chipping sparrow, and so on—in reality are buntings, slimmer birds than the house sparrow. They, too, have nine primaries. The house sparrow's secondaries number six; the tertiaries, small and hard to count, three; and those of the alula, three. The main tail feathers total twelve; the upper tail coverts, nine; and the lower ones, seven.

To a close observer these, and the other outercoat feathers of an adult male house sparrow, combine in the spring breeding season to produce a subtle, variegated design of colors, mostly sundry tones of gray and brown. The design is diversified indeed. The crown of the head and the nape of the neck are bright ashy gray. They are bordered on either side by a long chestnut streak extending from back of the black-encircled eye down toward the shoulder. A small white spot appears in the chestnut streak just behind the eye below whose black mask lies a large pearly space. The shoulders and back display broad stripes of black and chestnut or rusty brown and buff. The black chest splotch runs upward to join the black mask around the eyes, while the rest of the breast and underbody are buffy gray. The tail feathers are chiefly dusky or blackish brown with the edges lighter-colored. Upper tail coverts are tinged brown, the lower being brownish gray in the center. The closed wings look much like the back except for two distinct white wing bars. The wing lining appears grayish white. The bill in the breeding season is colored blue-black. In the winter the adult male house sparrow wears somewhat similar clothes. But, at that time of the year, it is tinged with more brown and less black above, and the black of its throat marking is partially obscured by whitish edges. In winter, and at all other times except during the breeding season, the bill is horn-colored.

The adult female sparrow exhibits no seasonal variation in appearance. On the back, the bird's coat is mainly brown, tinged with olive. The female lacks the chestnut streak and the white spot behind the eye and, of course, the black chest patch. Its breast and flanks are grayish brown with a buffy tinge, and the bill is much the color of the male's outside the breeding season. The young in first winter or first breeding plumage are much like the adults except that the males have their black chest feathers more veiled by white than do the adults.

In the northern hemisphere the house sparrow starts losing its feathers in late August. The molt is total, but gradual, ending in October. To the eye of an observer it is an unnoticeable process, causing the bird, which can fly and otherwise function normally at this time, no inconvenience. This is in contrast to the experience of ducks, geese, swans, coots, and many other waterfowl, which drop their flight feathers all at once after the nesting season and must hide among reeds and marsh plants until they can fly again. In the southern hemisphere the house sparrow has adapted over the years to the difference in seasons, and it breeds and molts there at the locally appropriate times.

The spanking newly acquired plumage of a male house sparrow has, at the ends of many of the feathers besides those of the throat patch, a grayish fuzz. This gives an indistinct hue to its pattern of colors. In the course of the months before the breeding season arrives these wear off, allowing the bird, when the time for mating comes around, to step forth in its most brilliant attire. Country birds in this resplendent condition, a famous ornithologist informs us, have sometimes been mistaken for a new species by birders from the city who are used to seeing house sparrows covered with municipal grime.

The reproductive cycle in the house sparrow, as in all birds, is the result of hormonal activity. Although temperature and sunshine-shade cycles are also involved, the process is started initially and chiefly by the increase in the diurnal light of spring. Apparently this acts indirectly on the reproductive organs, in both male and female birds, by stimulating the pituitary gland through the nervous system. The light is received most naturally through the eye. But its influence seems to be effective through the skin as well. For example, in a male house sparrow, tests with the eyes covered and a defeathered area of the skin exposed to light also produced testicular growth. The bird's responses to a series of hormonal commands, set in motion by the original one, lead to the entire spectrum of procreation: selection of a nesting site and building of the nest; courtship and mating; egg laying; incubation, including care of the eggs by shielding, rolling, cleaning, and covering; care of the young in the nest; and care and education of the newly flown young.

A male house sparrow's nest is his castle. He has a lifelong attachment to it and its site, just as he has a similar one to his mate. He defends the nest doggedly against all comers, even to engaging in occasionally fatal fights. He likes to line it with feathers, which he has been seen to snatch boldly from the flanks of larger birds, including pigeons. Or he will utilize hair that he filches after a swoop onto the back of an unsuspecting but immediately indignant dog. These additions make the nest snug during the winter when, in contrast to those of most other birds, it is still often occupied. When it is not, the sedentary male and his mate invariably return to it in the spring. The drive by a sparrow to take a nest site or nest object that it desires is strong. Such redoubtable antagonists as hornets have been routed from their paper home by a determined pair, which pulled out the combs and replaced them with grass and feathers. A young male house sparrow must build or acquire a nest before it can start courtship, a sort of adult initiation rite like those practiced by many primitive human tribes.

Courtship, as has often been noticed with both amusement and distaste by human beings, is a noisy procedure with much fluttering, rough-and-tumble acrobatics, and hot pursuit. Occasionally the female plays an unexpected role. One recent May, in a park in New York City, a male house sparrow was seen hanging in the air, his left wing held in a female's bill as she perched on the branch of a tree. He dangled limp in this undignified position, but continued his mating call of "cheep, cheep," his whole body vibrating gently. The pair remained thus for perhaps ten seconds, whereat he was released, flew to a branch near her, and recommenced more traditional wooing.

The house sparrow's egg starts with the yolk. This is formed in the left ovary of the hen. In her case, as in the case of all other birds, wild and domestic, barring the exceptionally rare individual, the right ovary, while present during the early embryonic development of the female chick, soon atrophies and becomes infantile, leaving the burden of egg production entirely upon the left member. By contrast, in our own species, both ovaries are operative; one ordinarily alternates with the other in taking charge during each monthly cycle. The mature avian yolk of whatever the species passes from the ovary into the oviduct, a tube at the lower end of which is the uterus. The oviduct acts as the assembly chamber for the other parts of the egg. There the albumen and the egg envelopes are added. The last are the two shell membranes and the shell. The shell membranes are the inner and outer translucent, papery sacs that surround the albumen and fit closely together except at the large end of the shell. There an air space exists to provide respiration for the embryo to come. The calcium for the shell is withdrawn from the hen's circulating blood and deposited as shell during the egg's stay in the uterus. The egg's coloration comes last, and it can be extremely varied. First the basic ground color is applied. This in the sparrow may be grayish white, greenish, or bluish, less often greenish gray or brownish. The overlay, normally always present, may be only a few—but then again, many—gray or brown dots, usually closely packed, varying from deep black-brown through many possible tone ranges to bright ashy gray. Typically the dots are most numerous at the blunt end. Albinotic eggs, usually the last in a clutch, are also known. Reptile eggs, of course, are pure white. The albinotic ones are thus regarded as throwbacks to the ancestral type. Glands in the uterus lay on the color. The main pigments are a red-brown called ooporphyrin; a blue-green, or oocynanin; a yellow, oochlorin; and a purplish red, ooxanthin. These, in the various avian species, combine to produce the wide range of tints that are to be found in birds' eggs. The colors are derived from the hemoglobin of wornout red corpuscles. These rupture, releasing the hemoglobin. This compound, which is dissolved by the blood, is carried by it to the uterine glands that do the deposition.

Nearly 80 percent of the egg-formation time is spent in the uterus, from which the egg, when complete, is expelled through the vagina into the nest. The last is a very brief operation. Laying normally takes place early in the morning at the rate of one egg a day. The egg's shape is elliptical, an average house sparrow's egg measuring about nine-tenths of an inch in length and six-tenths of an inch in width. It is a small egg, but at its typical bulk of two grams, it represents more than 5 percent of the body weight of the female. On the other hand, the single three-pound egg of the ostrich, the largest laid today, is equivalent to no more than 1.7 percent of the bird's body weight.

The sparrow's clutch of eggs, the number laid in a single set, is four at a minimum. But clutches of nine have been known. Usually the number is five or six. This is a rather large clutch compared with those of other birds. Penguins, like ostriches, lay one egg; the pigeon, never more than two. Partridges, however, may lay twenty. In line with other aspects of its redoubtable generative process, the house sparrow's ability to fashion eggs is formidable. In an experiment during which the egg produced each day was removed from the nest, the female valiantly laid a total of fifty-one in almost that number of days before giving up in what must have been considerable perplexity. This feat is all the more remarkable when it is realized that in less than two months the bird manufactured more than two and a half times its body weight in eggs.

Man has also analyzed the energy value of the house sparrow's tiny egg. It was compared with the much larger and better-known egg of the domestic hen. The energy value of 100 grams of a house sparrow's egg was found to be 116 calories; that of a hen's egg, consisting of an even mix of yolk and albumen, a little less than 200 calories. The comparison is not unfavorable to the house sparrow when it is realized that for centuries man has been engaged in increasing the food value of the hen's egg.

Although the male house sparrow occasionally covers the eggs, incubation is performed essentially by the female. The male has no brood spot, the featherless area on the breast against which the eggs are nestled. This provides the heat for their hatching. As with most small birds, the house sparrow's incubation is less than a fortnight, varying from twelve to fourteen days. During this time the eggs are sat upon and turned; toward the end, they emit vibrations as the developing embryo turns. Eventually, through the shell comes the sound of its soft cheeps.

The old saw that a bird lacks teeth overlooks the avian egg tooth borne by the embryo. The house sparrow embryo, as is the case with other avian embryos, leaves the shell through the aid of this accessory, a sharp, hard prominence at the tip of the beak. The embryo as the time for birth arrives is able to turn its head in the shell. The head is in the larger end of the egg. Pressing the egg tooth against the overhead cover, the little bird makes a slit in the shell in a circular pattern. Thrusting its head through this hole, it kicks back the larger piece of the shell and emerges as a nestling. As it does so, it makes a clicking sound by snapping together its mandibles, which are the upper and lower parts of the beak.

The newborn sparrow chick is flesh-colored and smoothly naked, lacking even natal down. Under the skin, which is transparent like pink chalcedony, the patterns of the feathers to come in the pterylae show as blue-dotted lines. The internal organs are clearly visible. The eyes are closed. So are the ears, just below and behind the eyes. The interior of the mouth is bright red. Toenails and bill edges are white, but the egg tooth and the center of the bill are horn-colored. For the first day and several days thereafter the adults feed the young on slender delicate flies and regurgitated, largely animal, food. To satisfy a brood of four, each parent must make about twenty trips to the nest an hour.

Change is rapid. By the end of the fourth day the nestling appears dark gray owing to developing feathers under the skin. The most advanced feathers are the primaries, where points have begun to protrude somewhat from their sites at the back of the wings. The eyes have opened. So have the ears, which show as small round holes. The mouth's interior brightness has toned down. The egg tooth has disappeared. The edges of the bill, no longer white, are now yellow.

The house sparrow nestling normally stays in the nest for fourteen to sixteen days. The greatest change in its looks takes place on the sixth or seventh day. Most of the feathers, which erupt in sheaths, come out then and many of the sheaths drop off. By this time the parents have stopped offering regurgitated food. Instead, large soft-bodied tidbits such as caterpillars are brought. By the tenth day the feather color pattern is shaping up. A wing bar is evident. Some males show the start of a black bib. The primaries, the main flight feathers, are now a little less than an inch long. At this stage, hard-shelled bugs such as beetles, which have been rendered eatable by battering or dismemberment, are added to the diet. By the fifteenth day, when the young are usually ready to fly, the body feathers are virtually all unsheathed. The primaries are nearly two inches long and most unsheathed, the bill is horn-colored; the inside of the mouth pinkish yellow, and the toenails much darker than at hatching.

During the period the young are in the nest, the feeding is shared by the parents. Late evening feeding, however, is done only by the female. This takes place for half an hour or so after the male has gone to roost. Then the female covers the young. The breeding season is the only time when the male retires before his mate. The rest of the year the reverse is true. Nest sanitation is also a dual responsibility, although the female handles most of this. As the young grow older, the parents place the feces at the nest entrance. This is a small hole located at the side of the structure if the nest is built in a tree or shrub. If the nest is crammed, as it often is, into the crevice of a building, the entrance is a hole placed in the sheer face of the exterior. This arrangement prevents the cowbird, a parental lazybones, from victimizing the house sparrow. The cowbird easily lays its single egg in the open cup-shaped nest of a warbler, vireo, true sparrow, or other small bird when the owner is not present. Then it covertly departs, leaving the unknowing host to hatch and care for its large, ungainly offspring, ever with sad results for the smaller indigenous brood. A house sparrow nestling, however, does sometimes die in the nest from other causes than the presence of an outsized cowbird chick. When this occurs the male removes it, carrying the remains in its bill, clutched at the juncture of the wing and body. Occasionally, also, an early tragedy occurs. Now and again a newborn fails to kick itself adequately out of the broken shell. The female then, following the normal procedure of getting rid of the shell, sometimes, apparently not noticing the young one, drops both the chick and the shell outside the nest, with fatal consequences for the former—a textbook case of throwing the baby out with the bath water.

As the time to vacate the nest approaches, the young more and more crowd the entrance. Departure time is usually in the morning, sometimes quite early. If all brood members are approximately the same size, they exit more or less together. But often this is not the case. Brooding starts before the clutch is complete, and thus hatching can occur over several days. In that event the smaller birds leave the nest a day or two after the larger. All are normally strong on the wing and, once out, it is next to impossible for a human being to catch one. Following the leave-taking, the fledglings are fed for several days by the adults. When some are in and some are out of the nest, the parents divide the task. Within a week after quitting their cradle, the young can feed themselves. There is a strong bond among them. They tend to join in loose flocks with other juveniles and drift away from the birth area, a move that in a sedentary species has the genetic benefit of preventing creation of an inbred population. The flocks seek food in waste areas supplied with weed seeds or in grain fields. If grain fields are nearby, they are a prime attraction. Later in the summer, when, with the waning of diurnal light, the breeding urge has passed, the young are joined at their gatherings, particularly at grain fields, by adult birds. The house sparrow would rather eat grain than anything else. Since an adult, ornithologists estimate, consumes six to eight pounds of food annually, the presence of numbers of them near a grain field can cost a farmer dearly.

In this country the house sparrow typically raises two or three broods a year, rarely four. Occasionally, however, more have been suspected, and even credited, to the species—seven in the Deep South being the maximum reported. Normally the span for breeding runs from spring to late summer, ending shortly before the molt, a development that definitely puts a temporary end to procreation. A brood period has been given as forty days, an interval that would keep a pair busy from early April to early August. But sometimes at the opposite pole from the inhibitory molt, a couple jumps the gun, the mating drive being what it is in *Passer domesticus*. For instance, a nestful of healthy young, as has been previously noted herein, was successfully reared in the frigidity of a Utah January. And this kind of precocious start is not necessarily unique. In Santa Fe, New Mexico, a house sparrow's nest containing five fresh eggs was found on December 12. The region admittedly is not as far north as Utah, but the occasion seems notable, nonetheless. And at Ottawa, Canada, which is surely boreal enough, a newly laid egg was found as early as January 18, while in Middlesex, Ontario, a young bird was seen during the last week of February. So conventional patterns of house sparrow breeding do not always obtain.

The house sparrow's determined urge to populate the world with its kind shows in other ways. One is devotion to its young. Dr. J. Denis Summers-Smith, a British observer and a leading authority on the house sparrow, reports the experience of a colleague: "A pair of sparrows was seen regularly flying up to the ventilation grilles situated in the walls of a house about a foot above the ground over a period of three days; investigation showed they were feeding through the grille a young sparrow that had fallen down the cavity wall. A hole was made in one of the grilles and the young bird came out and flew away strongly with the adults—it had obviously fledged a few days previously. The surprising thing is that the parents had been able to locate it through the grille and had not deserted it when it would not follow them."

And from a nineteenth-century issue of the *Zoological Journal of Great Britain* comes this: "A pair of sparrows which had built in a thatch roof of a house at Poole were observed to continue their regular visits to the nest long after the time when the young birds take flight. This unusual circumstance continued throughout the year; and in the winter a gentleman, who had all along observed them, determined on investigating its cause. He therefore mounted a ladder and found one of the young ones detained a prisoner by means of a piece of thread or worsted, which formed part of the nest, having become accidentally twisted around its leg. Being thus incapacitated for procuring its own sustenance, it had been fed by the continued exertions of its parents."

A bird of worldwide range like the house sparrow has, just as does man, individuals of differing dimensions at various localities inhabited by the species. For example, a typical adult male house sparrow of the eastern United States weighs a shade over an ounce, or the approximate heft of a silver dollar. Its length from point of beak to tip of tail is six inches, and the wing spread nine and a half inches. English and European house sparrows, on the other hand, are smaller.

The bones of the sparrow, wherever the individual may be found, are hung from the several dozen articulating vertebrae of the spinal column. They are light, the larger ones being actually partially hollow with very little marrow in order to make them even lighter. These last members are connected with numerous air sacs inside the bird's body. On the intake of breath, which in a house sparrow normally occurs more than 100 times a minute, the air goes from the lungs into the sacs and thence into the hollow bones. Exhalation then occurs. The continual repetition of the process allows the sparrow to take in much more air than would be the case if it filled only the lungs alone. The consequent heavier oxygenation of the blood furnished by the procedure fuels the great activity the bird exhibits and accounts for its normal temperature of 106.7 degrees Fahrenheit, more than 8 degrees in excess of man's.

At the upper end of the spine is fixed the delicate, but tough, skull supplied with large holes for the sparrow's relatively sizable eyes. The bird's brain, comparatively sizable also, lies to the back of the skull. Suspended from the middle part of the spinal column is the rib cage. To the top of this the bones of the wings are attached, on which flesh and flight feathers grow. The shaft of each primary and other flight feathers has at the bottom part a quill, which is hollow, and at the top the rachis, which is solid. From both sides of the rachis extend what we think of as the actual feather, the soft, silky membranes that look like solid sheets of matter. These, however, are in fact composed of manifold thin, parallel sections called barbs that are tightly linked to each other as though they had been zipped together, the joinery being performed by many interlocking hooks termed barbules that lie along the barbs' edges. The arrangement turns the vane of the feather into a surface solid yet pliant. The contour feathers, the ones that cover the body, in general have only fluffy barbs that don't interlock; these grow on the inner part of the rachis. Under them are wispy inner-coat feathers named plumules as well as the filoplumes that help keep the sparrow warm.

On the front of the rib cage is mounted the breastbone with its protruding keel sticking out like a prow. On either side of this are attached what, for the size of the sparrow, are its very heavy and powerful flight muscles. In all birds that fly, these tend to make up a considerable proportion of the body weight. They work the wings and control all flight movements, guiding the bird this way and that through the air by manipulation of the wings, which in the house sparrow are short, blunt, and pliable, allowing it to dart through small openings in bushes or buildings. They contrast with the long, narrow, flat, swept-back wings of the swifts, swallows, and falcons, which, with the sweepback preventing drag and providing high-speed stability, are ideal for the long rapid flight the house sparrow does not need. The sparrow's wings, on the other hand, which are deep-cupped, allow quick, high lift and good flight control, being highly efficient for its required short movements at moderate or low speed.

When flying at its usual pace, a house sparrow moves its wings thirteen times a second, a rather low count compared with the chickadee's twenty-five per second or the ruby-throated hummingbird's more than fifty. But it is several times more than the wing motion of the great horned owl, whose normal rhythm is three times a second. The top speed of a house sparrow in flight is usually given as thirty miles an hour, the characteristic figure for most of the smaller song birds, a group that thus is credited with going only half as fast as the hummingbirds' sixty miles an hour, a rate that permits these tiny avians to vie with the mallard duck, widely recognized as a species remarkably swift on the wing.

A report on house sparrow flight speeds at various places around the world was published in 1955 by Colonel Richard Meinertzhagen of the British army, a source often quoted on the flight speed of birds in general. He measured and then proceeded to describe bird flight speeds in articles in ornithological journals. In this country Meinertzhagen used a stopwatch and clocked the progress of certain house sparrows. When pressed, he said, these traveled at twenty-eight and thirty-five miles per hour. In the United Kingdom, using an automobile speedometer, he found sparrows on two occasions to be flying at thirty-three and thirty-five miles an hour. Again with a speedometer at another place in the United Kingdom, his reading was twenty-four miles an hour. Finally in Kashmir, with a stopwatch, he took counts on three migrating flocks and found them to be going at from thirty-three to thirty-five miles an hour. These last sparrows were exceptional individuals, being part of one of the only two populations of the species known to migrate regularly. The first group of these birds spends the winter months in India. They travel northward in the spring over the passes of the Himalayas to regions in Asia on the other side of the mountains, there raise only a single brood, and at the onset of cold weather return to India. The second population to the west of these does more or less the same thing but winters in Pakistan.

A decade after Meinertzhagen's report on the speed of the house sparrow, other measurements were taken with quite a different result. In the middle of the 1960s, a graduate student at Northern Illinois University went for two summers into the woods in northern Michigan and there studied bird speeds. He borrowed and used a device developed by a staff member of the American Museum of Natural History in New York City especially for the purpose of timing the speed of bird flight. It was a radar unit operating on the same principle as the kind used by police to spot speeding motorists. It was, naturally, a more scientific instrument than the devices Meinertzhagen had employed. At the end of two summers, the investigator discovered that the house sparrow was among the slowest of the seventeen species of birds he timed, going merely between sixteen and nineteen miles an hour. If the rader unit was used properly, previous estimates of the house sparrow's speed obviously have to be revised—provided, that is, that the northern Michigan birds involved were not a disgusting troop of dawdling drones.

The house sparrow's bill, the heavy, husky beak of a seed eater, is half to two-thirds of an inch long, considerably stouter than that of the song sparrow and other true American sparrows or, more properly, buntings. A strong bill with sharp sides is needed to cut through the tough coat of a seed. The digestion of such woody material is· aided by the gizzard, located at the lower end of the stomach. The interior of its thick, muscular walls has a lining of heavy, ridged plates that grate and tear to pieces the more resistant items of the diet. The food goes from the mouth through the upper half of the gullet into the crop, a pouch where what's been eaten can be held until the stomach, under the lower half of the gullet, is ready to accept it. Stomach acids help digestion before the gizzard goes to work. From it, the food passes through the duodenum and small intestine, an organ with many bends through whose walls nutriment is mainly assimilated before the waste leaves the body through the cloaca.

Birds lack a fifth toe. The arrangement of those that remain —three, four, or in the case of the ostrich, two—varies. The house sparrow has four toes, three pointed forward and one back. These balance the bird nicely on the ground or can be used to grip a branch firmly. By means of a handy physiological mechanism, the bird can go to sleep on its perch without fear of falling. As the leg muscles relax in slumber, a joint in the lower leg responds by bending. This tightens a tendon along the leg, causing the toes to grip the branch more tightly. A locking system keeps the apparatus in effect until the bird wakes.

The house sparrow's legs and feet are brown. Both are covered with scales, a heritage from reptilian ancestors of times past. The sparrow's form of surface locomotion, incidentally, is a hop. It doesn't run like the robin or walk like the starling. The hop is an ideal gait for moving in branches. Among other things, the sparrow is fond of bathing in sand, dust, or water. The object is not only cleanliness but also the curbing of lice and other body parasites. In bathing, in whatever medium, the bird tilts forward on its breast, flirts up the material with its bill and forward-dropping wings, and in obvious pleasure, snuggles down into its bath. The extent to which it will go to acquire a bath is illustrated by the following story. The action took place at a fountain and pool in downtown Baltimore. Harvey Brackbill states: "On the flat rim of this pool, covered by water to an ideal depth, sparrows were accustomed to gather and bathe. One day the pool was drained, leaving the birds with only some steep-sided bowls on a surrounding wall as watering places. From the rims of these they could lean forward and bathe their heads and shoulders, but the water's depth quite precluded complete baths in normal fashion. The birds got their baths nonetheless. To wash their hind parts they turned around and tipped slightly backward. And to wash their backs and underparts generally they flew very low across the water, dipping down into it one to several times on the way. Some contrived even better baths by swimming flutteringly the whole way across the bowls." So keen is the sparrow's desire to bathe that, somewhat like the members of the Polar Bear Clubs in this country, it has been observed ducking itself in water from melting snow. It also likes to sunbathe, especially in winter, when, finding a safe place, it ruffles its feathers to admit the solar rays and lies motionless for minutes on end. In hot weather, to cool off, the house sparrow cannot depend on sweat glands because it does not have any. Instead, it seeks what shade it can find, raises its feathers to lessen the heat around the body, and, like a dog, pants, opening its beak wide and evaporating water from its throat. In the searing heat of Death Valley, California, whither it penetrated early this century by hitching rides on empty incoming mule-hauled borax trains, the house sparrow adopts these techniques to make itself more comfortable in an environment whose peak midsummer temperatures may exceed 120 degrees Fahrenheit in the shade.

Of the five senses belonging to man, at least four are possessed by the house sparrow. One, the faculty of smell, is debatable. Most birds do not seem to have it, or not in any great measure. The great horned owl, for example, without flinching a mite, will consume a reeking skunk. The assumption is that were smell important the nostrils would be at the tip of the beak where they would do most good. Those of the house sparrow are, instead, located at the opposite end. This is the case with most birds. An exception is the flightless kiwi of New Zealand. A shy, nocturnal creature the size of a hen, it uses a long slender bill to probe in soft ground for worms and grubs. The sense of smell does seem to be employed by the kiwi. Its nostrils lie at the tip of the beak.

Vision is excellent in the house sparrow, as it is in birds in general, bird vision being by far the keenest in the world. The house sparrow, which sleeps during the dark hours and forages by day, has a relatively smaller eye, black in the case of both sexes, than such nocturnal species as the owls. Nevertheless, as is true of all birds, its eyes, when compared with the size of its body, are larger in scale than those of any nonavian animal. Its vision is supplied by light-sensitive rod and cone cells at the back of the eyeball behind the lens. The cones delineate objects in bright light and are directly back of the lens. The rods, which come into play when light lessens, are above them. In front of the rods and cones are tiny drops of yellowish oil. They act as filters and are helpful in allowing the house sparrow to look through the blue light of a haze. If it wishes, the house sparrow can move its eyeballs independently, looking up with one and down with the other. The human eye is an excellent machine. In the fovea centralis, the area of the cones and of the sharpest sight, man has about 200,000 cells per square millimeter. The house sparrow has about twice that number.

The house sparrow's hearing is also very good. Its range is not as wide as man's, but is adequate for all the sparrow's needs. The scale applied to the measurement of sound waves is cycles per second. Man's hearing range lies from 16 up to 20,000 cycles a second. How much of this very wide spread can be heard by any one person fluctuates greatly. To a degree, this may be true of the house sparrow as well. Its ear, like ours, has outer, middle, and inner sections. A feature of its inner ear is an apparatus connected with six planes that lie within different regions of the head. Thus, no matter how the bird turns its head, one or more of these planes with its apparatus for hearing is in a position to detect sound. This is true no matter what gyrations the bird may be engaged in, either on the ground or in the air.

A few years back two investigators at Cornell tested house sparrow hearing. The researchers found their own hearing was between 20 and 16,000 cycles per second. The house sparrow logged in at between 675 and 11,500 cycles per second. Thus, in the low and moderate range of sound, man hears better than the house sparrow—about two octaves better. However, the house sparrow figures meant that it hears all the sounds it normally makes, the low-pitched tones having little or no significance for it. As regards the upper end of the spectrum, that is now in question. A later study has put the upper limit of house sparrow hearing at between 18,000 and 20,000 cycles per second.

Touch is a sense very well developed in the house sparrow. The slightest contact with its feathers is immediately noticed. The quills, one ornithologist has pointed out, act as long levers to tell the skin if anything has moved them. The bird can also feel extremely faint vibrations of the ground or of any object on which it is perched, causing this wary creature, if it feels danger approaches, instantly to take alarm and fly off.

Taste, the final important sense of the house sparrow, is clearly present, but probably not as important to the bird as the sense is to us. Its existence can be seen, of course, when the bird spits out an unpalatable insect. But the operation of taste is hampered by the sparrow's method of eating. It swallows its small pieces of food whole after lubricating them with saliva. Thus the chewing process, which produces much of our sense of taste, is absent. In tests conducted on the taste of seed eaters, among which is the house sparrow, investigators discovered that these species are not sensitive to bitterness, even of an extreme order. The birds were given food soaked in solutions of both quinine and picric acid, which they ate without hesitation. The researchers assumed that the acrid nature of many seeds causes these species to disregard bitterness. However, seed eaters are fond of sweet things and, the experimenters concluded, can detect sweetness at the same degree of dilution that we can. House sparrows eat flowers, and one reason, some ornithologists believe, is to obtain the nectaries. Geese, on the other hand, dislike sweets. If, when expecting food, they are given a sugar lump, they will accept it and then quickly drop it.

An interesting correlation is to be found between the relative size of a bird's organ of vision, the eye, and the time it arises in the morning and retires at night. The length of daily activity, it turns out, is longer for the species with larger eyes. As illustration, an observer in England, checking this relationship, reported that the robin, an insectivorous bird with a large eye adapted to foraging in faint light, got up and sang, on the average, thirty-four minutes before sunrise, when the light was still dim but bright enough for it to see bugs. The principally granivorous house sparrow, on the other hand, with a smaller eye, is, like most seed eaters when in a temperate region, a late riser. Its time of waking during the period under review averaged almost seventeen minutes before sunup. In the evening the sequence was reversed. The house sparrow roosted early and the robin later.

The house sparrow possesses all the requisite equipment of a songbird. But what is generally heard from it is only its monotonous "cheep, cheep." Chirping usually at a rate of one call every two seconds, a most uninspiring performance to human ears, the male may, in the excitement of seeking a mate, up this rate to two calls every one second, hardly an improvement as far as human beings are concerned. In the wild state the young birds hear only the cheep and its sundry and minor variations—"chirp," "chweep," "chee-rup," and so forth. Hence that is what they perpetuate. Only rarely in nature is the house sparrow known to alter this. One such instance was reported some years ago in Minnesota in the month of September by Tilford Moore: "I heard a male in the honeysuckle beside my bed actually sing today. He was uttering the usual harsh chatterings of his kind, but about once a minute he'd substitute a short song for a squawk. The song was a thin and squeaky but rather pretty one, with tut-tut at beginning and end. Not a warble, it varied over several notes, was rather like an incomplete song which I have heard from a white throat."

However, such a performance is extremely uncommon. On the other hand, the sparrow's singing qualities in captivity were recognized as early as 1717. In that year a book was published in England giving melodies for teaching to house sparrows and other caged birds. In this country recently, one such caged sparrow, which had not been taught, was known by its owner "to warble for three minutes on end, stimulated by running water or the piano." In fact, when raised by man, the house sparrow's otherwise humdrum voice may become an instrument of generous range, as witness this report from Dr. Dayton Stoner of one household pet: "This unique sparrow possessed various types of vocal ability, which he utilized to express insistence concerning certain kinds of food, absence of the cage cover at night, general well-being, disgust and the like. Moreover, he acquired a remarkable proficiency in singing ability through the medium of two canaries which were his companions—in separate cages—for about six years. His imitations of the 'rolling' notes of the one and the 'chopping' notes of the other were so well done as to deceive even his mistress." The imitation of canaries by captive house sparrows is a common occurrence in the somewhat narrow field of caged-bird literature. The sparrows quickly pick up their neighbors' songs, forget them if removed from the canaries, and rapidly regain them when once more put within hearing distance.

Mimicry is the word for this song borrowing. Many birds are superlative mimics. Perhaps the greatest is the parrot. Long before the white man came to South America, the Indians there domesticated parrots and taught them to talk. In the last century, Baron Alexander von Humboldt, the great German naturalist, the founder of the modern science of physical geography, heard in the Amazonian jungles a parrot speak a dead language. It had been reared by a tribe, all of whose members had since been killed.

House sparrows, too, have been known to speak words. The eminent authority on caged birds, Johann Matthaus Bechstein, M.D., tells in his classic work, *Cage and Chamber Birds*, of a clergyman in Paris who had two house sparrows, father and son, which he taught to repeat the fourth, fifth, sixth, and seventh commandments in Latin. Bechstein adds, concerning the birds: "It produced a highly comic effect, when in quarrels over their food, one of them would gravely admonish the other—'Tu ne voleras pas' (Thou shalt not steal)." Bechstein, by his enumeration of the quoted commandments, shows that the clergyman was either Roman Catholic or Lutheran. Two ancient traditions, both of Hebrew origin, divide the commandments. One is embraced by the Roman Catholics and Lutherans; the other by the rest of the Protestant sects and the Orthodox communion. In the Decalogue accepted by the latter, the prohibition against stealing is the eighth commandment.

Ornithologists assume that virtually no small wild bird such as the house sparrow succumbs to senility. The rigors of existence for such creatures are severe. House sparrows fortunate enough to gain adulthood have a life expectancy of, it is believed, on the average, three or four years. Yet they are tough stock. With a little luck, their diminutive, hardy physiological machines will run in nature for several times that long. In June of 1944, for example, a member of the Department of Biology at Kent State University in Ohio banded a number of young sparrows. In October of 1957, two, both males, were caught and killed in traps two-fifths of a mile from the site of banding. The bander was eventually notified of the demise of these thirteen-year-old birds, but because, unfortunately, the carcasses had been destroyed, he could not determine from autopsy the birds' state of health at the time of death, information science would have doubtless found quite interesting. In England, a captive house sparrow, removed from the perils of woods and fields, lived twenty-three years.

Obviously, with the house sparrow's daunting fertility, there must be great mortality somewhere along the line from the egg on or the world would be overrun with house sparrows. Simple arithmetic reveals this. Depending on which ornithologist is read, the house sparrow usually has three to seven broods a year, in which the egg clutches vary from three to nine. Even allowing for a goodly, if presently unknown, proportion of sterile eggs and dead hatchlings throughout the house sparrow's worldwide range, each parent pair must produce many new sparrows every year whose total, if surviving merely a year or more, would mean a superabundance of house sparrows. Consequently, although the phenomenon may be quite unnoticed by man, many, if not most, of the young and a portion of the older birds, as well, must die. If one wishes to consider data from a limited section only of the bird's range, rather than the worldwide picture, some facts are presently available. Not long ago sparrow life-expectancy figures were worked out for Great Britain by Summers-Smith, the well-known British observer. He found that in his country the annual number of broods was one to four, with a mean of a little over two. The eggs in a clutch went from three to seven, with a mean of slightly more than four. Almost three-quarters of the eggs hatched and, again, almost three-quarters of the hatchlings fledged and flew. This gave a breeding success of approximately 50 percent. The figure is obtained, of course, by multiplying the percentage of hatching success by that of fledging success. However, Summers-Smith discovered that there was a high death rate among the young, inexperienced sparrows. Using personal observation and the recovery of birds banded as nestlings, he learned that of 100 that leave the nest, barely half live through the first month. Furthermore, the numbers of the youngsters, from one cause or another, diminish substantially over the next eleven months. Predators such as cats, hawks, and owls, along with the speeding automobile, find them a much easier target than their elders. At the end of a year about 12 percent is still alive and ready to breed. With a complete population of birds, young and old, considered from one April to the next, Summers-Smith, once more using personal observation and the retrieval of banded birds, discovered that there was essentially no annual increase in sparrow numbers. The 293 birds counted in the first April had, by the following August, expanded to 569. This was the population sample's high point. By December, however, the tally had fallen to 373 birds. Thereafter, each month the total dwindled until by April it was down to 303 individuals, only 10 birds more than the survey had started with. Since the survival rate of any animal is known to fluctuate from year to year for a number of reasons, such as food or predator scarcity or abundance, weather severity or the opposite, and other pertinent factors, Summers-Smith's figure of only a 3 percent increase in the census would be considered as indicating a stable population. For the whole of Great Britain, Summers-Smith estimated a sparrow total of almost 10 million.

This, however, is only a tiny fraction of those to be found in the Old World. For the continent of Eurasia, of which Great Britain is a part, a report contained in a scholarly tome, *Granivorous Birds in Ecosystems*, published late last year by Cambridge University Press, places the average population density in the house sparrow's Eurasian range at 422 birds per square kilometer. According to the map accompanying the report, the range covers some 55 percent of Eurasia's more than 330 million square kilometers, making a total there, if this estimate is correct, of more than 62 billion sparrows.

The oldest ancestor of the house sparrow so far discovered, a creature that lived 150 million years ago, is a bird the size of a smallish crow, named archaeopteryx. Its toes were arranged like those of the house sparrow—three in front and one in back. Thus it could easily perch on the cycad fronds that grew in the Mesozoic forests in which it lived. Or it could step along over their floors hunting food, probably small animals. The name means literally "ancient winged," from *archaeo-*, a Greek combining form denoting "ancient," and *-opteryx*, a second Greek combining form meaning "winged." The reason for the somewhat truncated designation was that the first evidence of archaeopteryx was the discovery, in the middle of the last century, of a well-preserved impression of a feather in slate beds of Upper Jurassic age in Bavaria, Germany. Before long, however, nearby and from the same formation, three more or less complete fossilized skeletons were found, the impressions of whose feathers matched that of the original one. As a consequence, archaeopteryx is now usually translated along some such lines as "ancient winged thing."

In due course, the fossils of earlier birds may be unearthed, showing more clearly the transition of birds from reptiles, which is the class of vertebrates from which the birds developed. But, at the moment, archaeopteryx is the most ancient representative of the root stock from which are descended all present birds, as well, of course, as those many species, now extinct, that appeared subsequent to archaeopteryx. The multiplicity of feathered forms, large and small, that have descended from archaeopteryx —or whatever was the true ancestral avian form or forms—is permitted through the workings of the complex process known as evolution. The same mechanism, for example, in the world of dogs is responsible for such different-looking animals as the Irish wolfhound, on its hind legs more than seven feet tall, and the tiny chihuahua, which can be easily held in a lady's hand. Both dogs—and all the intermediate dogs—trace their lineage back to a common domesticated caninelike ancestor.

Because of the proximity to its forebears, archaeopteryx unsurprisingly displayed certain reptilian features. Its beak, for instance, had dinosaurlike teeth, which would allow it to hold and tear the flesh of small animals. Its meaty tail was long like that of a lizard, although it bore feathers. And at the end of the wing bone there were three claws. These, ages earlier, would have been on the foot of a front leg, which, by archaeopteryx's time, had been modified to a wing. Nevertheless, despite these reptilian hand-me-downs, archaeopteryx was a true bird. It possessed feathers, the true test of a true bird, and these were more or less like those of today. Furthermore, scholars in general believe that it was a warm-blooded creature, as all birds are. This characteristic confers a tremendous biological benefit. The earlier developed vertebrates—the fishes, amphibians, and reptiles —were, and still are, encased in an environmental straightjacket. The most mobile and the furthest advanced, the reptiles, which alone are not chained to water, are still, nevertheless, the slaves of temperature. For they do not have the self-heating and self-cooling systems of the warm-blooded birds and mammals. As a consequence, they cannot be active in the winter and are excluded from many of the colder parts of the globe. The house sparrow, on the other hand, can exist, and exist without evidence of undue hardship, at places like Churchill, Manitoba, high up on the shores of Hudson Bay in winter temperatures that may drop to minus fifty degrees Fahrenheit.

For the next 100 million years following the period of the Upper Jurassic—a span that takes us out of the Mesozoic era into the Cenozoic, the most recent major division of geological time —birds were in the process of becoming more and more like birds. Although every detail in the picture is not clear, by the time of the Eocene epoch, some 50 million years ago, many of the larger birds were already, from the appearance of their fossil remains, much like modern forms. The smaller ones, again from their fossils, joined their larger fellows at least by the following epoch, the Oligocene, including, it is believed, examples of weaverbirds belonging to the genus *Passer*. By the next epoch, the Miocene, 12 million to 25 million years ago, representatives of *Passer* were certainly present. Their small bones and tree-perching habits made their remains less likely to be preserved than those of larger water and land birds, but fossil specimens of this genus were found in France in beds of Miocene age. The best present ornithological judgment is that the birds which furnished these remains spread to Europe from their putative continent of origin, Africa, including the one that was—or was to be—the house sparrow. Africa is the continent, also, where the house sparrow's eventual unwilling symbiont, man, probably also first evolved, rising up the ladder of time from earlier hominids. His emergence took place about 2.5 million years ago. By that time, however, contrary to the still somewhat apelike aspect of the forerunners of our own species, the forerunner of the house sparrow is thought to have been very much like the bird's trim self of today. Later, during the four ice ages of the Pleistocene, the relatively recent epoch that started 2 million years ago, the house sparrow must have backed and filled in its new territory, advancing to the north as the ice retreated, retreating to the south once more as the ice advanced.

Some 25,000 years ago, as the glaciers in the northern hemisphere were at last withdrawing, the Pleistocene epoch was considered to have ended. The epoch named Recent, in which we are now, began. It was during this time that the house sparrow made its intimate present connection with man. The glaciers in Europe and Asia unquestionably moved very slowly as they retreated northward. But the area above and to the east of the Mediterranean Sea had been sunny and mild for some millennia by 10,000 B.C. By then the wandering hunters and gatherers, who were the human beings of the period, began in southwest Asia to collect and to cultivate the seeds of cereal grasses, as well, of course, as to eat the seeds of the mature plants. By 8000 B.C., archeologists believe, real farming had been begun, well before what we label today as the epoch of history. Sedentary people living in what is now Iraq were responsible for this. The region was then, and is now, right in the range of the house sparrow. The bird, perched in protective shrubbery, may have watched the cereal planting with bright little eyes. Then and there it may well have started considering the advantages of sedentary life near grain fields as opposed to an uncertain, footloose nomadic one.

At any rate, as farming spread, the house sparrow, judging from its present habits, may be reasonably assumed to have done the same, hot on agriculture's trail. Southwestern Iran had farms by 7500 B.C. In another 1,500 years, the practice of tilling the soil had spread through Asia Minor to the Greek archipelago. On the basis of one piece of evidence, we can presume the house sparrow was actively present in Asia Minor wherever crops were produced. In the southern part of Iraq, in the fertile valleys of the Euphrates and Tigris rivers, arose the flourishing urban civilization of Sumer. The Sumerians, around 3000 B.C., invented cuneiform writing, which many scholars believe was the first written language. Thus some 5,000 years ago began the era of history. The wedge-shaped characters on some of the baked-clay writing tablets berate small birds, very likely sparrows, for their habit of devouring grain. Scholars today are uncertain whether the references actually concern sparrows or locusts. Both can come in swarms and both may be eaten for food, characteristics that certain of the passages note. Perhaps some of these refer to one plunderer and some to the other. In any event, it seems clear that the granivorous sparrow, probably in typically large numbers, inhabited the area around Sumer at that time. It was present, too, west of there, in the Holy Land. It is mentioned at various places in the Bible. In the pre-Christian version of the Old Testament, translated from the original Hebrew, the word "sparrow" appears in Psalms 84:3: "Yea, the sparrow hath found an house." (King James text). The word "sparrow" was originally *zippor*, the generic Hebrew term for bird. The Greeks, however, turned it into *strouthos*, their word for "sparrow." Did the Greeks, one wonders, know something additional? In the New Testament, whose earliest *known* written rendition was set down in Greek, the verse of Matthew 10:29 (King James text) goes: "Are not two sparrows sold for a farthing?" There the Greek diminutive *strouthia* is used, meaning "little sparrow."

Of course, the original authors of the cuneiform tablets and the Bible were not ornithologists. Thus, one cannot be absolutely sure today that the Sumer birds and the *zippor* or *strouthos/ strouthia* were house sparrows. But there are some positive indications that they could have been. First is the archeological evidence. Fossil remains place the house sparrow, or its forebears, in the Holy Land long before the Bible was written. A few years back in a cave in the Judaean hills near Bethlehem fossilized parts were found of two upper portions of the beak of a bird scientists call a primitive form of the house sparrow. This extinct bird, *Passer predomesticus*, is believed to have lived more than 400,000 years ago. Accordingly, the stock was in the area long before the present time, remaining there until, ornithologists today believe, it began its close association with man at the start of the age of agriculture. Another point is the grain-eating practice described by the Sumerians. Unarguably, this is the house sparrow's principal dietary habit. And if more of the verse of Psalms is read, the text has a growing man-connected flavor: "Yea, the sparrow hath found an house, and the swallow a nest for herself, where she may lay her young, even thine altars," suggesting birds that were living in, or near, man's structures. Biblical Jerusalem, of course, was a city. And there were others then, too, in the Holy Land and in Sumer. These factors—the archeological evidence of the early presence of house sparrow stock in the region; the presence in the region of agricultural man to whom presumably the bird was then, and certainly is now, closely attached; the region's contemporary supplies of grain, the house sparrow's main food staple; the existence in the region of cities, in whose structures house sparrows like to nest; and, finally, the bird's known fecundity, which would have produced an observable population —especially when taken together, contrive a reasonable case that the house sparrow was the bird being talked about in Sumer and in the Bible.

As long ago as the first half of the first century A.D., an early zoologist of the area did, in fact, positively identify the house sparrow as living there. He was Alexander the Myndian, a native of the town of Myndus in southwestern Asia Minor, who was noted for his writings about animals, especially birds. He differentiated the house sparrow from its near relative and look-alike, the tree sparrow. Both sexes of the latter display a black vest, but a smaller vest than that which the male house sparrow wears.

As the practice of tilling the soil advanced slowly but steadily through the Balkans and from there into the cool woodlands of central Europe, the house sparrow tagged along, dogging the footsteps of the farmer, until it occupied just about as much of the arable land of Europe as he did. Summers-Smith believes it arrived in Great Britain before the Roman occupation. By that time it was well established. As agricultural man in the island progressed northward, carving out farms and building towns in the undeveloped terrain, the sparrow went along, too. This is the pattern, the pursuit of man into his cities and farms, which the bird has elevated to a fine art, one that has enabled it to attain its awesome cosmopolitan range.

The house sparrow's success in what has ever been a highly competitive world is attributable in considerable part to its physical and mental endowments, mental being not too ambitious a word perhaps to use for its cerebral responses. These shortly will be discussed. But first the physical side. The sparrow is inordinately hardy. Several years ago a number of them underwent a series of rigorous tests. Their heart rate, temperature, and breathing were monitored in an environment whose oxygen content, decreased by the use of a vacuum pump, gradually became extremely low. This was to simulate high-altitude conditions. Unconditioned man normally suffers respiratory distress at a 10,000-foot altitude. Conditioned human beings who live at an altitude of 17,000 feet, the loftiest known to be occupied today, can work at no higher than 18,000 feet. This, according to the results of the tests, would be a piece of cake for the house sparrow. The senior researcher reported that the house sparrow is apparently equipped to survive thousands of feet above the tallest mountain on earth. Among the reasons, spotlighting only its heart action, are these, given in an excerpt from the published data: "The House Sparrow has a stroke volume which may be double the mammalian maximum and a cardiac output that is triple that of man and dogs. This combination of increased stroke volume and cardiac output enables the House Sparrow to transport oxygen in relatively large amounts even with low arterial blood oxygen tension."

As for intelligence, the house sparrow's brain is relatively large, more than half again as big, for instance, as that of a similarly sized mammal, the meadow mouse. The house sparrow's brain is usually 4.5 percent of its body weight; that of the mouse, 2.8 percent. To give another example, a lizard's brain is only approximately 0.55 percent of its body weight. A house sparrow uses its organ well. It learns quickly to tell what is important and what is not. Perhaps association with man, who is, of course, a consistent producer of new situations, has something to do with this. For instance, a sparrow one day turned up in an ornithologist's garage. But instead of fluttering about the ceiling and windows, as a house wren had done when caught the week before, it flew to the floor, cased the situation, and cannily crept out a crevice under the door. Other signs of brainwork are these. The sparrow will dip a hard crust in water to soften it before eating. Or, if no water is present, hold it firmly in one claw; this gives a pecking efficiency far greater than can be achieved by chasing the crust loosely over the ground. Perhaps the clearest tribute to the sparrow's mentality was contained in an article published several decades ago in the *American Journal of Psychology*. Among the conclusions reached were these: The house sparrow's method of learning is trial and error; it profits very rapidly by experience, its own or, through imitation, the experience of others; it has great powers of concentration, confining its efforts strictly to the matter in hand; it has a persistence that is striking; its highly developed sense of caution is by no means senseless because it prudently examines from a distance any new or strange object for danger; in an interval of eight days between tests, it showed little, if any, loss of memory; perhaps it owns the ability to count or, at least, a very nice sense of position; and, finally, when tested with food boxes whose fastenings were suited to the bird's structure and also with the device known as the maze, the sparrow's rate and method of learning were quite comparable to those of other higher animals, including monkeys.

The house sparrow in nature is definitely known as a wild and wary bird. But its intelligence permits it to adapt to, not fight against, enforced captivity. Caged-bird literature over the years contains many tales of sparrows that have made peace with unnatural situations—such as wearing a neck bell at its owner's whim and seeming to feel lost without it, or at a signal returning to its cage from outside its confines. One feathered internee even lived so long that its physical powers faltered. Thereupon it broke the universal house sparrow rule of surface locomotion by hopping only. Instead, the invalid switched to walking like a starling, which is a far less taxing method of getting around. If acquired early enough, and given tender care, a house sparrow will evidently conceive of itself, not as a bird, but as a human being. Mr. and Mrs. Alfred S. Jones of Washington, D.C., a few years back found a baby house sparrow near death on the pavement, so newly hatched as to be still naked. It would have been one of the many young birds that fail to survive their first month had it not been for the Joneses' care. They took it home, fed it many times a day with warm milk forced down its throat with a medicine dropper, and, as it grew and thrived, named it Joe. The bird's voice was like that of the resident house canary. On outings to the park it rested on Mr. Jones's shoulder. It occasionally scratched the ground during these visits before returning to its elevated human perch. But it never flew to trees or shrubbery or paid the slightest attention to other sparrows. Apparently it regarded them as an alien race. It consumed milk, toast, meat, eggs and breadcrumbs. It required a humming lullaby in Mr. Jones's cupped hands before retiring, and it rode for hundreds of miles on the steering wheel of the Joneses' automobile.

Man in his poetry has written about the house sparrow in at least eighteen languages—Arabic, English, French, German, Greek, Hindi, Hungarian, Italian, Polish, Rumanian, Russian, Spanish, Turkish, Urdu, and the four languages of Scandinavia. In English, among those in the antisparrow category is this extract from a poem by William Cowper, the eighteenth-century English rural poet:

> *The sparrow, meanest of the feathered race,*
> *His fit companion finds in every place,*
> *With whom he filches grain that suits him best.*

In opposition to this characterization is the following stanza from a work by Barry Cromwell, a little-known British bard of the last century:

> *On my window's ledge*
> *I'll leave thee every morning some fit food*
> *In payment of thy service. Doth he serve?*
> *Aye, serves and teaches. His familiar voice,*
> *His look of love, his sure fidelity,*
> *Bid us be gentle with so small a friend,*
> *And much we learn from acts of gentleness.*

One of the longer poems on this topic, *The Sparrow*, is an effort of forty-seven short stanzas by William Carlos Williams, the contemporary American poet. *The Sparrow*'s first verse begins:

> *This sparrow*
> > *who comes to sit at my window*
> > > *is a poetic truth.*

and ends with the subject's death beneath the wheels of an automobile. This conclusion, as given in the following lines of the poem, seems perhaps quite fitting for as ordinary but indomitable a creature as *Passer domesticus*:

> *Practical to the end,*
> > *it is the poem*
> > > *of his existence*
> *that triumphed*
> > *finally;*
> > > *a wisp of feathers*
> *flattened to the pavement,*
> > *wings spread symmetrically*
> > > *as if in flight,*
> *the head gone,*
> > *the black escutcheon of the breast*
> > > *undecipherable,*
> *an effigy of a sparrow,*
> > *a dried wafer only,*
> > > *left to say*
> *and it says it*
> > *without offense,*
> > > *beautifully;*
> *This was I,*
> > *a sparrow.*
> > > *I did my best;*
> *farewell.*

What does the future hold for the house sparrow, one of the most intelligent of the 8,500 full avian species alive today?
A continued expansion of range and population in all proba-

bility. Whether it now holds one-quarter or one-half the area inhabited by man on this planet, or whether it is advancing into new territory as has been stated at the rate of twenty miles a year —or more or less than twenty miles—its progress into new terrain seems unlikely to halt. Alaska, still not part of its turf, will doubtless be included before long as the bird proceeds, as it now is doing, up the coast of British Columbia. The northern parts of South America, in those sections where man is present, also will eventually almost surely see the house sparrow. So will areas as yet uninhabited by the bird in south central Africa, western Australia, and, in due course, it seems safe to say, the archipelago of Japan. The house sparrow finds ways of getting places suitable to its way of life.

In addition, within this highly plastic organism itself, there are signs of further advances, if they can be called that, in the bird's way of doing things. It is holding, and adapting itself stubbornly and successfully to, the ecological niche that exists in our rapidly changing cities, using its intelligence to find new nesting sites in today's functional architecture and new food sources amid the steel and concrete of today's urban environment—efforts that are quite different from those required in the rural settings it also still occupies. Quoting from the experiences of A. H. Scott, an English aviculturist, Summers-Smith notes instances of possible psychic groundbreaking within the bird itself: "Scott bred house sparrows for a number of years in a large planted aviary. He ringed a brood of four young sparrows one day but they were rather young and he was doubtful whether the rings would stay on. When he went to check the following day there was only one nestling in the nest. Further examination revealed that two of the nestlings were in another sparrow's nest about twenty-four feet away with two young birds that had previously been in the nest. The fourth young was found dead on the ground between the nests. The two young were taken over and reared by their foster parents. Scott is of the opinion that the adults had carried the young across after their nest had been disturbed. He was actually present in the aviary when the hen at the same nest dropped a live nestling of a subsequent brood when attempting to carry it across the aviary towards an unoccupied nestbox. Again this took place after he had just disturbed the nest by ringing the young. Scott reports other similar occurrences in his aviary . . . he suggests that the house sparrow may be evolving from the lowest stage of parental behavior (desertion) to a higher stage of activity—saving the young by attempting to remove them to an undisturbed nest." When it is recalled how house sparrows, in the wild, endeavor to succor and feed young ousted from the nest, it seems clear that in many individuals this higher form of parental behavior may be in the process of being incorporated in the genes. This is a development that, if it becomes part of the intrinsic nature of the species, will only add to the present formidable success of the house sparrow, a form of wild life that is already most breathtakingly successful in nature's complex and highly competitive world, whose manifestations are all too often overlooked by members of our technological society. It is a world much more fundamental than the transient one we have manufactured—enduring, ruthless, puissant, kaleidoscopic in its variety. It is a world in which the superior organism inexorably advances, *vide* the wily coyote extending its range. A persistent one in which—in the midst of our greatest metropolis—wildflowers respond to sun and rain. It is a powerful world in which scars on earth's surface remind us of the might of a past glacier whose like may come again. An often inscrutable world where a tree, once thought lost, emerges like a ghost from the shadows of time.

It is a world of beautiful trivia in which the sudden arrival in our temperate zone of an avian waif from Arctic seas shows that even the rarer works of creation can, at any time, burst unexpectedly upon our ken—something industrial science, with all its pomp and power, can neither evaluate nor foretell . . . but, without which, growing numbers of us here think our planet would be poor, indeed.